A

MANUAL

FOR

CHILDREN'S
DELIVERANCE

Frank & Ida Mae Hammond

SPIRITUAL WARFARE SERIES
VOLUME VI

A Manual for Children's Deliverance,
Frank & Ida Mae Hammond
ISBN # 0-89228-078-6

Copyright ©, 1996
Impact Christian Books, Inc.
332 Leffingwell, Suite 101,
Kirkwood, Mo. 63122
Tel. 314-822-3309
Orders-only line: 800-451-2708

Scripture quotations are taken from the *New International Version* of the Bible, unless otherwise indicated.

Printed in the United States of America

TABLE OF CONTENTS

GRATEFUL ACKNOWLEDGMENT
IS MADE:

To **Shirley Smith** of North Little Rock, Arkansas, for her very helpful contribution to this book. In 1981 the Lord called Shirley Smith to the ministry of "Watchman" and showed her many things that Satan is using to deceive our children.

Shirley has generously shared with us her research exposing the evil influence of toys, games, music and television upon the lives of today's children. Many of Shirley's "watchman" insights and warnings are reflected in chapters nine and ten.

To our proofreader, **Phyllis Jennings**, for her invaluable help in perfecting the manuscript.

Frank & Ida Mae Hammond

INTRODUCTION

This book concerns deliverance for children. The term "deliverance" as used here encompasses both the process and the result of one's liberation from demonic bondage. Deliverance is achieved by driving out evil spirits by the authority of the name of the Lord Jesus Christ.

Since some who read this book may not be altogether familiar with the scriptural grounds for deliverance, we wish to devote this introductory chapter to acquainting our readers with the basic tenets of deliverance. We also recommend other books that we have published on various aspects of deliverance. A list of these books is given at the end of this volume.

Deliverance Basics

The Gospels of Matthew, Mark and Luke abound with accounts of Jesus casting demons out of people. A major part of His earthly ministry was devoted to deliverance. His purpose in becoming man, dying on the cross and conquering the grave was to defeat Satan in our behalf. "The reason the Son of God appeared was to destroy the devil's work" I John 3:8.

Jewish religious leaders were amazed at the authority Jesus exercised over demons. They said, "He even gives orders to evil spirits and they obey him" Mark 1:27. He did not use incantations or any sort of paraphernalia; He merely spoke to these real yet invisible beings and they obeyed Him. "He drove out the spirits with a word..." Matt. 8:16.

Furthermore, Jesus trained The Twelve plus seventy-two other disciples and commissioned them to cast out demons.

> He called his twelve disciples to him and gave them authority to drive out evil spirits...The Lord appointed seventy-two others...The seventy-two[1] returned with joy

1

and said, "Lord, even the demons submit to us in your name." Matt. 10:1; Luke 10:1, 17

Prior to His ascension into heaven, Jesus commissioned His Church to preach the Gospel throughout the world, confirming the Word with signs following. The first sign mentioned is deliverance: forcing demons to depart from a person in the Name of Jesus.

> And these signs will accompany those who believe: In my name they will drive out demons.   Mark 16:15-20

The Believer's Authority

[1]Believers in Christ have been entrusted with spiritual "power of attorney": authority to act in the absence and interests of Another.   All authority in heaven and on earth belongs to Jesus (Matt. 28:18), and He has given us complete power over Satan and the demonic kingdom. Even though we cast out demons, the devil has no power to retaliate or harm us in any way. Jesus said:

> I have given you authority to trample on snakes and scorpions, and to overcome all the power of the enemy; nothing will harm you.   Luke 10:1

Deliverance is for God's people

When a Gentile woman requested deliverance for her little daughter, Jesus refused her and declared that deliverance is "the children's bread" Matt. 15:26. Only after she expressed faith in Him did He comply with her request, saying, "Woman, you have great faith! Your request is granted" Matt. 15:28. Likewise, all others, who through faith in Christ become God's children, are qualified to receive "the children's bread".

A lost person rarely seeks or submits to deliverance. He has no interest in the things of God. His eyes are blinded and his heart hardened.   He is dead in trespasses and sins, following the ways of Satan

---

[1]Some manuscripts have "seventy"

2

through, "the ways of this world and of the ruler of the kingdom of the air" Eph. 2:1. He cannot benefit from deliverance because, without filling himself with the virtues of the Holy Spirit, the evil spirits can come back seven times stronger than before.

> When an evil spirit comes out of a man, it goes through arid places seeking rest and does not find it. Then it says, "I will return to the house I left." When it arrives, it finds the house unoccupied, swept clean and put in order. Then it goes and takes with it seven other spirits more wicked than itself, and they go in and live there. And the final condition of that man is worse than the first.
>
> Matt. 12:43-45

Can a Christian have a demon?

No distinction is warranted between Christians and non-Christians having demons; the New Testament makes no such distinction. Our hearts are grieved by those who contend that Christians cannot have demons, thus robbing believers of a valid ministry purchased for us by the blood of Jesus.

Can a Christian be demon possessed? Herein lies much of the confusion. "Having" demons and being "possessed" by demons are entirely different matters. Possession denotes ownership. A Christian belongs to Christ. He has been purchased by the precious blood of Jesus (I Cor. 6:19,20).

THE KING JAMES BIBLE, and a few other versions, have translated *daimonizomai* as "demon possessed", whereas the word correctly means "to act under the control of demons. Those who were thus afflicted expressed the mind and consciousness of the demon or demons indwelling them (Luke 8:28)."[2] Thus, Christians can be influenced and controlled by demons who indwell them, but demons cannot

---

[2]*Vine's Expository Dictionary of New Testament Words*, W.E. Vine, Riverside Book & Bible House, Iowa Falls, IA, p.283.

3

"possess" or own a Christian. Demons dwelling in Christians are trespassers without legal rights; therefore, they are subject to eviction in the authority of the Name of the One who has redeemed such believers unto Himself by His blood (I Pet. 1:18).

Some have questioned, "How can an evil spirit dwell in a person who has the Holy Spirit within him?" The answer is made clear by remembering that "your body is a temple of the Holy Spirit" I Cor. 6:19. The Temple in Jerusalem had three parts: Outer Court, Holy Place and Holy of Holies. The presence of God dwelt solely in the Holy of Holies.

The three compartments in the Temple correspond to man's tripartite being: body, soul and spirit. For the Christian, the human spirit corresponds to the Holy of Holies, which is the dwelling place of The Holy Spirit. The Holy Spirit desires us to submit every area of our "temple" to His control. Other temple areas include the mind, the emotions, the will and the physical body.

Jesus found defilement in the Jerusalem temple; however, the money changers and the merchants with doves and cattle were not in the Holy of Holies, but in the outer courts of the temple. Jesus proceeded to "cast out" all who defiled the temple (Matt. 21:12). This is a perfect analogy to deliverance. Defilement is not in the spirit of a Christian but in the "outer courts" of his mind, emotions and body. There can be defilement in the Outer Court while the presence of the Lord remains in the Holy of Holies. Jesus is highly displeased with such a condition. He wants His temple cleansed and every defiling demon cast out.

Balance Is A Key Factor

Not every problem is demonic. For example, Jesus healed people without casting out demons. Not every demonic problem is exclusively demonic; there is also flesh that must be crucified. Dead flesh and unclean spirits are co-dependents; you rarely find one without the other. Any one who receives valid deliverance cannot expect to retain his deliverance apart from disciplined living. His tongue, mind, emotions, will, physical appetites, finances and his spirit-man must remain rigorously disciplined. "Like a city whose walls are broken down is a man who lacks self-control" Prov. 25:28. The enemy has ready access to the life of one whose walls of discipline are broken down.

Why Seek Deliverance?

Why should a person want deliverance for himself? Is needing relief from torment, defilement, addiction or compulsive behavior a valid motivation? We know the Lord wants us to be free from every oppressive bondage, but Christlikeness is always the highest motivation. We should hate everything in us that detracts from Christlikeness and gives advantage to the devil.

Prerequisites for Deliverance

The Word of God lays down three absolute prerequisites for those who seek deliverance from oppressing evil spirits. First, one must repent of all sin. Repentance is a firm resolve in the Lord to forsake sin and turn about to walk in the ways of God. Ongoing sin in one's life is an open invitation to demons. Yielding to sin is yielding to a "whom", a person: namely, the devil.

> Do you now know that to *whom* you present yourselves slaves to obey, you are the one's slaves *whom* you obey, whether of sin to death, or of obedience to righteousness?
> Rom. 6:16 (Italics ours)

Second, there must be unqualified forgiveness toward all others no matter what they have done, how many times they have done it, or whether they continue to offend. Forgiveness of oneself is also mandatory. Anyone who has any reservation about

5

forgiving any other person is turned over to tormenting demons until he pays the debt of love's forgiveness.

> In anger his master turned him [the unforgiving servant] over to the jailers until he should pay back all he owed. This is how my heavenly Father will treat each of you unless you forgive your brother from your heart. Matt. 18:21-35 (Brackets ours)

Third, there must be a complete separation from every association, no matter how casual, with the occult, cults and Eastern Religions. This separation includes the destruction of all books and paraphernalia associated therewith. (Deut. 7:25-26; 18:9-13; Acts 19:19-21).

Judged By Its Fruit

One day a group of proud, pious Pharisees challenged the validity of Jesus' deliverance ministry. They accused him saying, "It is only by Beelzebub, the prince of demons, that this fellow drives out demons" Matt. 12:24. In the midst of a particularly pointed response, Jesus challenged His critics with these words:

> Make a tree good and its fruit will be good, or make a tree bad and its fruit will be bad, **for a tree is recognized by its fruit.**
> Matt. 12:33, (Emphasis ours)

Indeed, let deliverance be judged by its fruit! After two and a half decades in deliverance ministry on four continents, we have found that deliverance is a VERY fruitful ministry. The most dramatic and instantly recognizable fruit of deliverance has occurred in children to whom we have ministered.

Many parents who have brought children to us for deliverance have said, in effect, "Our child is not responsive to training, discipline or love". It is not unusual for all such negative traits to be completely reversed after only one thorough session of

6

deliverance. This change is tangible fruit of deliverance!

It is a tremendous benefit to children when, by casting out oppressing demons, those resistant to discipline become pliable; those who could not be cuddled are now receptive to touching love; the rebellious and stubborn become governable; the devious are made trainable in truthfulness and honesty, and the restless and agitated become peaceful. Consider the quality difference that deliverance can make in a person's life.

Parents, too, are greatly benefited by the changes that deliverance makes in a child, for many frustrations and hassles are terminated.

Each child that is born into this world is a unique individual. God has designed each one with a personality all his own. One of the greatest challenges parents face is training and nurturing each child so that the full potential of his special personality is developed and channeled in the ways of God. When evil spirits hinder or block this process, conscientious parents can become perplexed and discouraged.

Children are the most valuable assets that a family, church or society has. Our objective as Christian parents and ministers should always be to lead our children to love and serve Jesus Christ, so that they will not be captured by the Antichrist system of this world. We need every resource which God has provided. The employment of our spiritual authority over demons is a God-given resource, enabling us to bring and keep our children in the Kingdom of righteousness, peace and joy.

1

JESUS' MINISTRY TO CHILDREN

There are two accounts in the Gospels of Jesus healing children of demons. A study of these passages brings to light several foundation principles which give direction for children's deliverance.

The first account tells of a father who brought his son to Jesus. He had already taken his boy to the disciples, but they were unable to deliver him. Here is the scriptural account:

> The next day, when they came down from the mountain, a large crowd met him. A man in the crowd called out, "Teacher, I beg you to look at my son, for he is my only child. A spirit seizes him and he suddenly screams; it throws him into convulsions so that he foams at the mouth. It scarcely ever leaves him and is destroying him. I begged your disciples to drive it out, but they could not."

> "O unbelieving and perverse generation," Jesus replied, "how long shall I stay with you and put up with you? Bring your son here."

> Even while the boy was coming, the demon threw him to the ground in a convulsion. But Jesus rebuked the evil spirit, healed the boy and gave him back to his father. And they were all amazed at the greatness of God.   Luke 9:37-42

The second account is that of a Canaanite mother who came to Jesus on behalf of her little daughter who was suffering from demon oppression.

> Jesus withdrew to the region of Tyre and Sidon. A Canaanite woman from that vicinity came to him, crying out, "Lord, Son of David, have mercy on me! My daughter

is suffering terribly from demon-possession."[3]

Jesus did not answer a word. So his disciples came to him and urged him, "Send her away, for she keeps crying out after us."

He answered, "I was sent only to the lost sheep of Israel."

The woman came and knelt before him. "Lord, help me!" she said.

He replied, "It is not right to take the children's bread and toss it to the dogs."

"Yes, Lord," she said, "but even the dogs eat the crumbs that fall from their masters' table."

Then Jesus answered, "Woman, you have great faith! Your request is granted." And her daughter was healed from that very hour.

Matt. 15:22-28

Children Can Have Demons

The first truth that we discover from these two passages is that children *can* have demons. Neither of these parents had any problem identifying the source of their children's torment. How different that is from most parents' perception today. Most mothers and fathers would recoil in horror if someone suggested that their little ones were oppressed by evil spirits.

We are reminded of those days when the Lord was leading us into deliverance ministry. For us, it was a gradual process of comprehending for whom deliverance applied. At first we thought it was only for those who were deeply enmeshed in sin: the prostitute, the alcoholic, the dope addict. Next, we added the mentally and emotionally ill to our list of

---

[3]The Greek word *daimonizomai* translated "demon-possession" does not carry the meaning of ownership; "badly demonized" is a clearer rendering.

9

deliverance candidates. What a shock it was to us and those of our fellowship, when a visiting minister discerned and cast demons out of Ida Mae.

Then, after each adult in our fellowship had gone through a measure of deliverance, a young mother requested that we cast oppressing demons out of her little son. We recoiled at the idea. "Surely," we thought, "this is taking deliverance too far!" The mother insisted that she was sure that her little boy had demons. She pointed us to Matthew 15:21-28 where Jesus delivered the Syrophonecian's little daughter of demons. This convinced us that it is possible for a child to have demons, which gave us the faith to proceed. We cast the evil spirits out of the child, and his behavior improved.

Children are very vulnerable to the infiltration of demons. Why? Children are totally dependent upon others for their care and protection. Parents are the God-appointed, spiritual guardians of their children, yet too few parents are knowledgeable and vigilant in providing a spiritual covering for their children. (We will come to these matters in greater detail in another chapter.) When we recognize the gates through which demons enter, we can then understand what parents must do to guard their children.

Corrective punishment is a companion to deliverance. As Scripture puts it, "Folly is bound up in the heart of a child, but the rod of discipline will drive it far from him" Prov. 22:15. Along with the casting out of demons, a stubborn, rebellious child must sometimes be disciplined repeatedly and consistently. The goal is to bring the child to the point of self-discipline. Unless the flesh[4] is disciplined, the demon of rebellion and his companions will soon return.

---

[4]"Flesh" (Greek, *sarx)* is used in the sense of the power in man that opposes the working of the Spirit.

10

Detection Of Demons

(A second truth) derived from Jesus' ministry to the two children, is that the presence of evil spirits in children may be determined by what is happening to the children. The boy whose father brought him to Jesus exhibited symptoms of epilepsy. The father described the demonic symptoms as follows: "A spirit seizes him and he suddenly screams; it throws him into convulsions so that he foams at the mouth. It scarcely ever leaves him and is destroying him" Luke 9:39.

Such physical trauma in a child would motivate most parents today to seek treatment from a medical doctor. Jesus concurred with the father's diagnosis and "rebuked the evil spirit". The child was instantly healed and handed back to the father.

The Syrophonecian woman explained to Jesus how she concluded that her little girl was beset by a demon. She said, "My daughter is *grievously vexed* with a devil" (King James); "*cruelly harassed* by a demon" (Weymouth); "*seriously afflicted* with insanity" (Lamsa); "*in a terrible state* - a devil has got into her" (Phillips) Matt. 15:22.

Jesus did not challenge the mother's conclusion that her child was demonized. In fact, Jesus showed agreement with the mother when He declared, "You may go; the demon has left your daughter" Mark 7:29.

Some theologians have contended that Jesus simply accommodated Himself to the superstitious beliefs of the woman. No, Jesus did not play games with words. He who is Truth never agrees with error.

There are two ways to determine the presence and activities of demons: discernment and detection. Discernment is supernatural; a gifting of the Holy Spirit; the ability to distinguish between spirits (See: I Cor. 12:10). "Detection" is derived from the Latin word for discover. "Detective" comes from the same

11

root word. A detective is one who examines the evidence and discovers the truth.

If a child is stubborn, rebellious and untrainable it does not take supernatural discernment to know what spirits are manifesting. They are readily detected.

A woman who lived about twenty miles from us brought her infant daughter for deliverance. She said, "My little baby is just two weeks old, and I want you to deliver her of evil spirits." She explained to us that the RH factors between her and her husband were not compatible, and, at birth, the baby required a blood exchange. This procedure entailed the extraction of the infant's blood which was replaced with blood transfusions. Ever since the blood exchange, the baby had been nervous and hyperactive. She was not sleeping normally. There was a constant nervous jerking of her body.

The doctor had sent them home from the hospital with a prescription for Phenobarbital, with instructions to give the barbiturate to the baby. The mother said, "Something in my spirit just says that I cannot start my baby out on drugs." We agreed that her baby's vexations were symptoms indicative of the presence of evil spirits. We had not had any experience with such things, but we thought it possible that the trauma of the blood exchange could be the root cause of the child's affliction.

It was a precious deliverance. Ida Mae held the infant in her arms and quietly commanded a vexing spirit to go. The baby cried briefly and then became peaceful. A spirit of irritability was commanded to leave. Again the infant cried and then became quiet. This pattern of crying followed by peace, repeated itself over and over as demon after demon was commanded out.

A week afterward, the mother telephoned us. She reported that her baby was sleeping, and the nervous jerking had stopped. Through this experience, the

Lord confirmed to us that even infants could need deliverance.

Parents Take the Initiative

A third truth that surfaces in Jesus' deliverance for children is: Parents must take the initiative for their children. It should be obvious to all that a child is incapable of seeking deliverance for himself. The parent must bring his child to Jesus. The father in Luke chapter nine brought his son, and the mother in Matthew fifteen came to Jesus on behalf of her little daughter. The successful outcome of these two ministries should encourage parents to seek deliverance for their children. In multiplied hundreds of cases, we have seen deliverance bring peace to the child and rest to the parents. This, in itself, is a strong motivation for not neglecting children's deliverance.

When we announce deliverance services for children, we require that each child be accompanied by one, or preferably both, parents - or an official guardian. It is especially beneficial to have the father in attendance. The father is God's delegated "head" of the family, and evil spirits recognize his authority. Too, it is heartening to see fathers truly concerned for the spiritual welfare of their children.

Jesus Honors Faith

The fourth truth common to both incidents where Jesus cast demons out of children is: Jesus honors a parent's faith. Both the father and the mother who sought Jesus on behalf of their children exhibited faith in Christ.

The father first begged the disciples to cast out the epileptic demon, but they were unable. This failure did not dissuade or discourage that father. Persistent faith is evidenced as he pressed through a crowd of people and called out directly to the Master: "Teacher, I beg you to look at my son, for he is my only child" Luke 9:38.

Jesus was grieved that His twelve disciples were weak in faith, for He had given them power and authority to meet such challenges. He lamented:

O unbelieving and perverse generation...how long shall I stay with you and put up with you? Bring your son here.   Luke 9:41

Both those who minister and those who come for ministry must have faith.

The Canaanite woman, a gentile "dog" so far as the Jewish people were concerned, showed more faith than those who boasted that Abraham was their father. At first Jesus simply ignored her plea. Then, the disciples suggested that He send her away, but she kept crying after them. Even when Jesus declared to her that it was not proper to toss the children's bread to dogs, the woman persisted by saying, "Yes, Lord... but even the dogs eat the crumbs that fall from their masters' table" Matt. 15:27. Jesus was moved by the mother's tenacious faith; whereupon He replied, "Woman, you have great faith! Your request is granted" Matt. 15:28.

We, too, admire the faith of parents who let nothing stand in the way of their children receiving deliverance. We have seen parents take their children out of school, parents take off from work, families travel great distances and make other special sacrifices to obtain deliverance. We have seen how the Lord honors such faith by granting special anointing for deliverance.

2

WHEN THE WOMB IS UNSAFE

The devil is a strategist. He devises a plot and plan for each person whom he attempts to capture. How early in one's life can he begin to execute his plan? We are convinced that he initiates his evil scheme the moment one is conceived in his mother's womb. No new life goes unnoticed by Satan. It is the devil's intention to destroy each life, if possible, or to cause as much harm as he can. Satan is called Apollyon[5], The Destroyer.

The devil's options are limited. He must operate within the bounds of his legal rights. In other words, he must have an opening before he can get into a person's life.

God's word exhorts us, "Do not give the devil a foothold" Eph. 4:27. How can the devil get a foothold in the life of a child still in his mother's womb? What would open that door of opportunity?

Inherited Curses
First of all, inherited curses give the devil a legal right. God has decreed:

> I, the Lord your God, am a jealous God, punishing the children for the sin of the fathers to the third and fourth generation.
>
> Deut. 5:9

Children are born with anywhere from a few to many curses due to "the iniquities of the fathers" Exod. 20:5. Parents, grandparents or great-grandparents have transgressed God's commandments, and the curse has passed down. Perhaps there has been idolatry, witchcraft, occult practices, incest, fornication, illegitimacy, adultery, bestiality or other transgressions

[5]See: Revelation 9:11

in the family tree. Unless these curses have already been disallowed, the atoning blood of Jesus accepted *and the demons of curse expelled*, then the devil has a right to perpetuate the curse to another generation.[6]

Pre-natal Rejection

What other right does the devil have? Phyllis, a young woman, approached us concerning deliverance for her child. She said, "My baby needs deliverance." Since she had no baby in her arms and was obviously pregnant, we queried, "Do you mean the one in your womb?" She said, "Yes" and began to explain why her unborn child needed deliverance.

When the baby was conceived, Phyllis did not want a child. She had since learned that rejection of a child in the womb creates an opening for a spirit of rejection to enter him. The baby was now at six month's term, and the mother had gotten her heart right with the Lord. She now accepted the baby and had dedicated him to God. She asked that we deliver her little one from the spirit of rejection.

Is a child in the womb subject to spiritual influence? "What about John The Baptist?" we recalled. "Hadn't an angel of the Lord appeared to Zacharias, the father of John the Baptist, and announced that John **'shall be filled with the Holy Ghost, even from his mother's womb'**"? Luke 1:15 KJ, emphasis ours. John's infilling of the Holy Spirit was evidenced when Mary brought salutation to Elizabeth, and the babe leaped in her womb.

Since the Holy Spirit can enter a person before birth, why couldn't an evil spirit also enter a person still in the womb? After pondering this scripture about John the Baptist, we agreed with Phyllis that her child could have a spirit of rejection, and we sensed that

---

[6]See: *The Breaking Of Curses*, Frank & Ida Mae Hammond, Impact Christian Books, Kirkwood, MO. 1993.

God was in her request. Ida Mae laid hands on Phyllis' abdomen, and the spirit of rejection along with other spirits were commanded to come out. The demons came out of the child through the mother's mouth with yawns and coughs.

After the child was born, we received a report that he was a quiet and peaceful baby who was very much loved. This child's tranquillity was in marked contrast to others who are rejected from the womb and who receive no deliverance. A child rejected from the womb is usually fretful, cross and irritable. He is prone to being stiff rather than relaxed in the mother's arms. He usually resists being held or cuddled.

This experience with Phyllis, along with many similar experiences, answered for us the question, "When is the proper age for a child to receive deliverance?" The answer: Any time from conception onward.

This experience also shored up our growing conviction that a baby still in the womb is not in a state of oblivion. That little embryonic person can be spiritually influenced in either positive or negative ways. If a babe, still in the amniotic fluid, can be wounded by rejection, he can also be nurtured by love. When should parents begin to love a child? Parents should begin openly to confess love for their child from the moment of conception. It is good to speak tender words of love and acceptance to a child throughout his nine months of development. It is indeed a mystery, but that little baby receives spoken love and feels wanted and secure.

Emotional Environment

The over-all emotional environment has an impact upon the developing child within the womb. Evil spirits are given ready access to a yet-to-be-born child through many kinds of negative factors in his outside environment. Many would deny that such influences are possible, but our experience has proven otherwise.

In cases where the conception is illegitimate, as in many teen-age pregnancies, there are usually many negative forces at work. For example, the unborn child is usually rejected by both the father and mother. The father may walk off, refuse to accept his child, press the girl to seek an abortion (to kill his child), choose not to marry the girl and deny all responsibility. This is utter selfishness. In his mind it is all the girl's fault for getting pregnant.

In other scenarios, the young woman and her family deny the father access to his child. They are in a state of humiliation and want to punish the young man in every possible way. All such factors send tremors through the womb that foster insecurity and rejection.

If there is talk of abortion or giving the child up for adoption, a wound occurs and demons enter. Abortion is the irreversible wound of rejection. In such cases there is no recourse for the child through healing and deliverance.

Adopted children are prime candidates for deliverance, although the adoptive parents dearly love the child. The wounds of rejection and abandonment have already occurred, and the devil has seized his opportunity. Thank God, there is deliverance in Zion!

A mother-to-be's emotional condition will also influence the fetus.[7] In other words, the baby will be vulnerable to the same kinds of emotional spirits that the mother carries -- such as fear, anger and depression. Therefore, it is important for the mother to be happy, confident in the Lord and healthy in her emotions.

---

[7]*Fetus* is from the Latin: "Act of bearing young; offspring". (Webster's Seventh New Collegiate Dictionary; G. & C. Merriam Co., Springfield, MA.)

Such factors in home environment as fighting, quarreling and loud music bear an effect upon the emotional health of a child. His nervous system can also be damaged.

The father should provide strong emotional support to the home environment through his love for both mother and child.

The Mother's Addictions

It is well known that children can be harmed physically from the addictive habits of the mother, and these may even be born with addictions. Infants of drug-using mothers go through painful withdrawal symptoms when the umbilical cord is severed and the drug stimulus no longer passes from mother to child. We have discovered some people who later in life became enslaved to alcohol, nicotine and other drugs due to the prenatal influence of mothers' addictions. The spirits had lain dormant for years, just waiting for an opportunity to seize control.

Birthing Complications

The very first commandment that God gave to man was, "Be fruitful and increase in number" Gen. 1:28. Needless to say, the devil hates mankind's fruitfulness in childbearing. Knowing this, when a birth takes place, all involved should be spiritually vigilant against all attempts of Satan to destroy life or to harm mother or child.

Frank recalls a day when he was notified that, Jackie, a young woman in the fellowship, was at the hospital in labor. When Frank arrived at the hospital the young woman's mother, Sue, was standing outside the room. She explained, "The doctor is in there now. He has determined that the baby is not in position for birthing. They are planning to do a Caesarean section." Neither the father nor the grandfather was present. Frank said to Sue, "Let's pray!" They agreed in prayer that the baby would turn and that there would be a normal birth. They rebuked the devil and commanded him to get his hands off the situation. Frank and Sue had scarcely finished praying when the door to Jackie's room swung open, and two nurses went flying down the hall pushing Jackie on a gurney. The doctor was right behind them. Sue called out after them, "What's happening?" The doctor answered over his shoulder, "The baby turned. We're taking the mother to the delivery room." Within minutes, the message came back: "It's a girl. Everyone is fine."

If this were an isolated incident, we probably would not give it a second thought. However, we have heard and read many similar testimonies. The ideal spiritual covering is realized when the "head of the woman" speaks into the situation. A husband/father has a God-given authority to speak life and blessing when the wife gives birth to his child.

3

PREPARING FOR DELIVERANCE

Preparing The Minister

The minister of deliverance may be a pastor, any other Church leader, a lay person or the parent of a needy child. Neither a theological degree nor a special title is required. What is needed are those who understand that deliverance ministry is biblically sound, know their spiritual authority in Jesus Christ, are empowered with the gifts of the Holy Spirit, have compassion for the oppressed, carry a special love for children, are willing to step out in faith and are not afraid of making mistakes.

Some people have a zeal for deliverance ministry. Zeal is commendable when accompanied by knowledge. The one infallible source of knowledge is the Bible. The most pertinent Scriptures are the Synoptic Gospels which convey to us how Jesus dealt with demons and how He taught, equipped and commissioned His disciples and His Church to cast out demons in His name.[8]

There are many resource books and teaching materials on the subject of demons and deliverance.[9]

---

[8]See: *Demons And Deliverance In The Ministry of Jesus* by Frank & Ida Mae Hammond, Impact Christian Books, Inc., Kirkwood, MO. 1991.

[9]When we were thrust into the ministry of deliverance in 1968, there were few resource materials to be found in Christian book stores. We soon became aware of the need for a guide book on deliverance. We approached two ministers who were prominent in deliverance work at that time, suggesting that one of them write such a book. Neither of these men had it in their spirits to write what we felt was so urgently needed. Whereupon, with only four years of experience under our belts, we undertook to write

One will be wise to judge each of these in light of Scripture.

It is ideal for one who is called to deliverance to be the apprentice of a proven deliverance minister. We realize that this is not always possible. The next best alternative is to work in conjunction with another person or small group of individuals who have an interest in deliverance. Husband and wife teams can be quite effective. We encourage ladies to keep themselves under pastoral, husband or other spiritual covering.

I (Ida Mae) recognize that I have been given a Divine commission and anointing for ministry to children. Over the years the Holy Spirit has taught me many helpful techniques for children's deliverance. As I share these methods, I pray that no one will use them mechanically or limit himself to what I have learned. I believe that the Holy Spirit will give others additional insights for effective ministry.

Undoubtedly, the best instruction to be had is in "the school of the Holy Spirit". We should not limit ourselves to what can be gleaned from the insights and experiences of others. There is no substitute for what the Holy Spirit reveals. Fresh insights usually come in conjunction with hands on ministry.

One should also covet and anticipate a flow of the supernatural gifts of the Holy Spirit. The gifts of knowledge, wisdom and discerning of spirits are invaluable to those who minister in deliverance.[10]

such a book. The result was *Pigs In The Parlor, A Practical Guide To Deliverance* which contains a chapter on "Ministry To Children". The devil tenaciously fought the writing and the publication of this book, and he still fights its translation into other languages. Nevertheless, we humbly acknowledge the blessing of God and the anointing of the Holy Spirit upon *Pigs In The Parlor*. Since the book's publication in 1973, it has helped many understand basic deliverance.

[10]See: I Cor. 12:8-10

Why are the gifts of the Holy Spirit so important? Tiny babies and small children are unable to give us factual information about themselves, so we are truly dependent upon the Holy Spirit to give us "keys" to guide us. If an infant is vexed, how can we determine the cause? We need skills comparable to a medical diagnostician.

I recall going to a diagnostic physician for help. As I waited in the examination room for him to come in, I noticed on the wall his diploma for veterinary medicine. I thought to myself, "What kind of doctor is this? Does he think I am a horse or a cow?" So, I asked him why he had such a degree. His explanation was quite informative. Animals cannot talk and convey their symptoms. The veterinarian is trained to diagnose without patient input; therefore, veterinary school provides excellent training for medical diagnosticians.

We work much like diagnosticians, except we rely upon what the Holy Spirit reveals to us. For example, a four-year- old boy was brought to me for ministry. His mother said that he was tormented by fear, but she was unable to pinpoint the root cause of his fear.

As I began to pray, the Holy Spirit gave me a mental vision of a rooster. I shared this with the mother. She said that they lived on a farm and had chickens in their yard. The mother recalled that one day a rooster had chased the boy. He was three years old at the time, and the rooster was almost as big as he was. The lad was seized with fear. That is when a spirit of fear entered him. So, the word of knowledge working through a mental vision provided the key for his deliverance.

On another occasion I was praying for a three year old boy. The Holy Spirit gave me the word "penis". I asked the father if his son had any problem with his penis. He said, "Yes, he pulls at it all the time and says, 'It hurts! It hurts!'" We determined that a spirit

23

of pain had entered at the time of circumcision, and the boy was delivered from the oppressing spirit.

Also, this little boy had been adopted. We were told that his biological father had a history of sexual promiscuity. We knew that it was important for us to break the power of the inherited curses that had passed down through the father's sins, and this was done.

We have found other spirits associated with circumcision. While praying for a five-year-old boy, I received a discernment on circumcision. I asked the mother, "Who circumcised him?" The mother exclaimed, "Oh, my! That pediatrician has been discredited and lost his medical license due to malpractice". The mother also informed me that the doctor was involved in the occult. "He mutilated my son's penis, and he has had problems with his penis ever since."

The mother and I broke the demonic soul tie with that doctor, and prayed for healing.[11] Later, the mother told us that her son's penis was healed, and he never complained about it again.

Preparing Parents

When parents are not familiar with deliverance, it is important that they be instructed concerning what to expect and how to cooperate. As a general rule, parents require more preparation for a child's deliverance ministry than does the child. Children's deliverances are, on occasion, quite demonstrative, and parents who do not understand the process may fear that the child is being mistreated or harmed.

We make it a practice to inform mothers and fathers that there can be considerable crying and physical struggle. It is not unusual for a child to become soaked with perspiration after forty-five

---

[11]See: *Soul Ties* by Frank Hammond, The Children's Bread Ministry. 1988.

minutes to an hour of flailing and writhing. During deliverance, a young child may plead for comfort from mother or father (usually the mother). Since infants cannot commit their wills to cooperate with the ministry, their fleshly natures get stirred up when demons are stirred up. This agitation of the flesh is desirable in young children's deliverances. We soon discovered that any comforting of a child's flesh during the time of deliverance enables evil spirits to hold on tighter and hinders the deliverance process.

It is very natural and proper that parents be protective of their children. God has designated them as spiritual protectors and providers. Fathers and mothers need the assurance that everything is being handled right in the Lord. The deliverance worker must take the necessary time to make parents feel comfortable with the ministry, bringing them to the place where they have confidence in the ministering person and confidence in the methods of deliverance.

When we sense, or even suspect, that a parent is uncomfortable with any aspect of the ministry, we always respect that concern by giving explanations and assurances. In a very few instances, parents have asked that the deliverance be discontinued, and we have always yielded to that request, trusting God for another opportunity.

When parents have experienced deliverance for themselves, they gain an understanding of what deliverance is like, and they are able to be at ease with ministry to their children. For this reason, we make it a priority for the parents to receive deliverance first.

Ida Mae recalls an early deliverance experience: a dramatic encounter with strong demons in a six-year-old girl. If you have read our book, *Pigs In The Parlor*, you may recall the following account:

The most graphic child deliverance I have ever had was that of a six-year-old girl. We will call her Mary. Mary's father came to us for deliverance. In the course of the interview he spoke of the difficulty he had in handling his daughter. He and his wife were divorced, and he was raising the girl. He said that she was a most difficult child to handle, being very stubborn, self-willed and rebellious. He was quite concerned since her nature caused him to become so excessively angry that he would punish her too severely. We told him that the girl needed as much deliverance as he, if not more, and insisted that he bring her to us.

Mary came to us directly from school a few days later. While I was explaining to her that I wanted to pray for her, she drank about a half a thermos of orange juice. She was very hyper-active, jumping on and off the church pew, absolutely unable, due to restlessness, to sit while we chatted.

I said, "Mary, your father tells me that you know there are bad spirits". Her eyes widened and she began to tell me very seriously how every night she had to make sure all the doors were locked before she could go to bed. When she got up in the night to get a drink or go to the bathroom she was afraid and had to know personally that all doors were securely locked. I said, "Yes, that is fear, Mary. You have demons of fear in your body. They make you afraid and I want to pray for you and make them leave your body. They have gotten inside you, and, when I pray, they will come out through your mouth and leave." She accepted my words with simple, child-like faith.

I asked her to come sit on the bench beside me while I prayed. She did, but she was so restless that I had to take her on my lap to keep her near me. She sat on my lap with her back toward me. I began to pray a prayer of faith and trust that Jesus was going to set her free. The Holy Spirit very plainly told me to keep my voice very quiet - lower than a conversational tone. Also, to consider every word hereafter that came out of Mary's mouth to be a demon speaking or to be demon inspired.

Then I began to address the demons. I said, "Now, you demons indwelling Mary's body, I want you to know that Mary is covered by the blood of Jesus through her father's relationship to Jesus. Just as the father in the days of Moses sprinkled the blood on the door post for the protection of the entire family, so is Mary under the covering of the blood. Demons, I also want you to know that Mary's father has heard and accepted the truth of God's word concerning you demon spirits. He knows now that it is you he has been struggling against and not Mary."

I became aware that Mary was whispering and leaned around to see if I could catch what she was saying. She was whispering, "I don't like what you are saying." I replied, "I know you don't like it, demons, because I am exposing you, and I have knowledge of you. Mary has been tormented by you from before she was born. While she was still in her mother's womb, some of you entered her. But God has said you cannot indwell her body any longer." Again the demon in Mary began to whisper, this time in very tight-jawed defiant words they protested, "I ....don't ...like ...what ...you ...are ...saying!". I was careful to keep my voice very quiet as I responded, "It's not going to get any better for you, demon, but worse because you are going to be cast out of her today. You are losing your home." At this the demon screamed out and again retorted, "I don't like what you are saying; now shut up!" I replied, "No, I shall not shut up but rather will continue to talk until you are out of her body."

I continued speaking to the demons, "Now, one by one you demons start manifesting yourselves, in the name of Jesus." Immediately Mary began to say in a whisper, "You don't love me; if you did you wouldn't be holding me." I answered, "That's right, *rejection demon*, you shut her off from love relationships. You make her think nobody loves her. You even make her think God doesn't love her. You are going to come out of her, rejection, in the name of Jesus." One by one the demons began to manifest their nature. They came so quickly I often only had time to name one and another would be to the surface.

The demons were making Mary struggle to get out of my lap although I was still able to hold her rather loosely in my arms. Eventually I had to resort to putting one of her legs between mine, thus holding her in a vise and bodily restraining her. The demon of hate put her face right up in my face with our noses touching and screamed, "I hate you." Still speaking quietly I addressed the demon, "Come out, *demon of hate.*" She began to scream, "I want a knife, I want a knife." I inquired, "What do you want with a knife?" The demon clenched Mary's teeth and said, "So I can kill you." "All right, you *demon of murder*," I commanded, "you come out in Jesus' name."

Next, Mary stood up, threw her shoulders back, placed her hands on her hips and retorted, "Nobody EVER tells me what to do!" I said, "*Defiance*, you come out!"

There was a distinct change in voice as the next demon spoke. It said, "I do only what I want to do." I said, "*Self-will*, come out." Then there was another change in voice. "You will never make me come out", said the new voice. "*Stubbornness*, you have to come out, too", I insisted. Mary then raised her hands like claws and lunged for my face; her eyes were protruding, and she was screaming. I said, "*Madness*, you come out of Mary in Jesus' name." She began to claw her hair and shake her head violently. I said, "*Mental illness* and *insanity*, come out." Next, I called for the spirit of *schizophrenia*. "You demons of schizophrenia, I call your hand. You bring out your two opposite personalities which you are establishing in her. One of you is rooted in *rejection* and *self-pity* and the other is rooted in *rebellion* and *bitterness*. Neither one of those personalities is the real Mary. I release and loose the real Mary to be what Jesus wants her to be." With this she clawed violently at me, scratching my arms, and lunging for me she bit a hole in my blouse. When she came up with part of my blouse in her teeth, she looked very startled as though she expected me to slap her across the face. I could tell it was the real Mary who was startled. I addressed the demons and said, "No demons, I shall not hurt Mary for ruining my blouse because I can separate her from you. Too long Mary has been punished in her flesh for the things you have done through her. You demons have gone virtually untouched. It's different today; you demons are taking the punishment, and Mary goes free." Mary looked relieved for a second, then the other demons began manifesting themselves.

Finally, after about twenty or thirty minutes of this deliverance procedure, Mary began to scream one long scream after another and beg to be turned loose. She would say, "Don't hold my leg! Don't hold my leg!" The Holy spirit gave me understanding that her flesh was now stirred up and that I should release her and have her sit on the bench beside me. I instructed, "Mary, I'm going to let you sit on the bench. Okay?" She was crying softly and said, "I don't like for you to hold me like that." I said, "Well, I'm sorry I had to hold you so tight, but the bad spirits were making you fight me."

29

I was always careful to put the blame on the demons. In her childish way, she seemed to appreciate that they were finally catching the blame instead of herself.

Mary sat beside me for a little while and was very still and relaxed. The Holy Spirit told me that I should now give the command quickly for the remaining demons to come out. I said, "Now, in the name of Jesus, I command all demon spirits remaining in Mary to come out. Come out now, in the name of Jesus!" Immediately Mary became sick at her stomach, and before I could reach a paper towel, she threw up a large ball of slime. It filled her little hands and mine. She looked up and faintly smiled and then just seemed to turn to peace all over.

Remember, at the beginning of this account, I stated that Mary was drinking a thermos of orange juice when she came for ministry. There was not a trace of juice in what she threw up. None of the slime came from her stomach.

Well, we sat there and talked for about fifteen minutes. Mary sat quietly relaxed, in contrast to the hyperactive nature she had shown earlier. Her father was astounded. He had watched the stormy deliverance with mixed and confused emotions. Unfamiliar with demon manifestation, and unable to distinguish the many different voices of the demons as my trained ear had done, Mary's father thought that the real Mary was being treated rather roughly and said that once it was all he could do to keep from interfering.

Though I have not personally seen Mary since her deliverance, I have received several good reports. Most say, "She's so different." "She just isn't the same." "I can hold her, and she responds to love." "You just wouldn't believe she is the same girl."

My eyes get moist even as I write this. The warfare was so tumultuous, and the peace afterward so beautiful. I could not keep back the tears. To God be the glory![12]

After the above account was published, the father and his daughter visited our home. It was a cold, snowy night, and we all sat visiting on the floor in front of the fireplace. Mary was peaceful. It took only the slightest correction from the father to control Mary's behavior. What a magnificent victory!

Well, that is how God established me in children's deliverance with a six-year-old girl. I was inexperienced and had no idea what I was getting into. Once I got into it, I knew that God had given me a special love and anointing for children's deliverance

One would think that God would initiate a person into children's deliverance with a nice, easy case; one where the child merely yawned the demons out. God seems to prefer to start his ministers out with difficult cases. I've heard other ministers tell about starting out with someone involved in witchcraft or some other highly demonized individual. God knows how to train His servants and keep them humble.

Mary's father brought her to me for deliverance. He was present when the deliverance took place. The importance of working together with the parents cannot be over emphasized. When we announce a deliverance service for children, we make it a requirement that each child be accompanied by his parents. There are situations where only one parent is available, and that is acceptable. A grandmother or a grandfather can bring a child for deliverance, if the

---

[12]Hammond, Frank D. & Ida M., *Pigs In The Parlor*, Kirkwood, MO, Impact Christian Books, Inc., 1973.

parents have given them permission, or if they have legal guardianship.

It is not acceptable for an aunt, for example, to invite her nephew or niece over to her house on the pretext of taking the child to a deliverance service, even though she knows the child obviously needs deliverance. We instruct people not to pick up the little "Dennis the Menace" in their neighborhood and bring him to the deliverance service.

Mothers have brought children for deliverance against the knowledge or approval of the fathers. If such a child is old enough to talk, he will probably go home and tell his father what he has experienced. It would be the natural thing for the child to do. Therefore, the mother should be aware of this possibility and be prepared to accept the consequences.

Parents and official guardians are responsible for their children's spiritual well-being. They must understand how demons got into their children and be committed to protect them from the evil spirits' return and from further invasion. Unless the parent or guardian assumes spiritual oversight for a child, there is little prospect of that child retaining the deliverance he receives.

However, there are sometimes exceptions to the rule that a child's deliverance must be ministered with the parent's consent. This policy is evidently not an absolute with God. I recall ministering to a twelve-year-old girl. Her parents had given permission for neighbor friends to take her to their church. She had accepted Jesus as her Savior and was attending our deliverance conference. She asked to receive deliverance. The neighbors felt it was unnecessary to seek her parent's permission since she was born again and was under their authority. It was a graphic and meaningful deliverance.

While I was casting demons out of Mary, the Holy Spirit impressed upon me that this girl did not have a good home environment, and it would be difficult for her to maintain her deliverance. He then instructed me to send the demons into a far country. I said, "I send you demons to Africa." Immediately the demons began to whine, "No! Too far! Too hot! Too far! Too hot." I've never been instructed to do that since. It was a special assignment, and we have not made a doctrine out of sending spirits to distant places.

I asked God for understanding to know why they were saying, "Too far! Too far!" I could understand "Too hot!", but why "Too far?" The Holy Spirit revealed that it would place the spirits under a different demonic principality within Satan's kingdom; a place of which they were not knowledgeable. They would not be experienced in the culture, and would not be able to perpetuate the generation curses with which they were familiar.

How Children's Deliverance Differs From Adults'
First, there is a difference in the level of communication. One cannot have a pre-counseling session with infants and small children. These little ones are totally incapable of explaining their problems and delving into the root causes of their need for deliverance. Therefore, the diagnostic procedure differs from that with teens and adults. The counselor must rely upon the parent or guardian of a child to identify tell-tale symptoms of demonization.

In the two scriptural examples cited in Chapter I, each parent told Jesus how their child was being affected by demons. The boy's father explained: "A spirit seizes him and he suddenly screams; it throws him into convulsions so that he foams at the mouth" Luke 9:39. The Syrophonecian mother exclaimed, "My daughter is grievously vexed with a devil" Matt. 15:22 KJ. So, the parents described their children's needs.

33

In addition to information supplied by parents, the counselor must also rely upon the gift of "discerning of spirits". A wise counselor will closely observe a child's behavior before and during the actual deliverances. By so doing, he will often detect symptoms of demonic influence. For example, demons often betray their presence in a child through the child's rebellious and stubborn attitude, fretfulness, crying, mother-clinging, need for a security blanket, thumb sucking and other less-than-ideal conduct.

Second, there is a difference in the level of cooperation. The counselor can expect no help by appealing to the will of a one or two-year-old child. Tots a little older than this can actually set their wills against the deliverance minister. Parental authority and disciplinary measures are sometimes required to gain the necessary cooperation.

Third, there is a difference in comprehension. Explanations are not appropriate when children are too young to understand what is being said and what is happening. There is no need to launch into a prolonged discourse upon how the "works of the flesh" lead to demonization, and how flesh and demons become intertwined. However, the deliverance minister himself must make the distinction between flesh and demons, and deal with flesh and demons as separate entities which are intermingled in a child's personality and behavior. This distinction can be made without a child's comprehension or cooperation.

For example, the minister will be aware of demons' ability to nestle down and conceal themselves when a child's flesh is comforted during the deliverance procedure. Those who minister to children will discover that deliverance is made easier when a child's flesh is deprived of comfort by the simple technique of taking a child from a parent's arms and having someone else hold him.

Fourth, there is a difference in maintaining deliverance. While adults and teenagers are responsible for self-discipline and spiritual growth; children remain vulnerable to demons and are incapable of protecting themselves or of waging aggressive warfare. Parents must fill the role of spiritual watchmen and maintain deliverance for their little ones.

Preparing Children And Youths

The initial preparation of children for deliverance should be done by the parents. The best preparation is the example set by parents who receive deliverance first. When Junior sees the change in his father, the fairer and gentler way in which his father treats him, and the absence of bad character traits, that boy will begin to see the advantage in getting rid of bad spirits.

Make deliverance a family affair. If it is good enough for Mother and Daddy it's good enough for Junior. (Why should our little ones and hassle with demons until they become old enough to take their own initiative and seek deliverance for themselves?) Pastors and parents, let's not neglect the "lambs" that God has placed in our care. Jesus has a question and a command for you and for us: the same words with which He challenged Simon Peter: "Do you truly love me?...Feed my lambs" John 21:15. Literally, deliverance is "the children's bread" Matt. 15:26.

The ideal is for an entire family to have deliverance together, because the devil works in relationships to cause friction, division and all sorts of hurts. Many a family has been brought into victory through deliverance. Wherever there are problems in a home, we encourage and exhort the parents to take the spiritual initiative to receive God's help. There is no need to remain in trouble; Jesus died to provide victory.

Also, the fear element is taken away when parents lead the way. After all, it may sound awesome and monstrous to a little tike if he is informed that he has demons, and someone he doesn't know is going to cast them out of him. Put yourself in his place, and you can begin to appreciate the importance of some sensible preparation. It will certainly be comforting to the child to see Mom and Dad lead the way.

Remember, however, that when you have put the child at ease, you have not comforted whatever demons are in him. The more light that is shed on evil spirits, the more excited they become. When they perceive that they have been discovered and are about to be cast out, they will often betray their presence.

For example, Frank recalls the following episode with a five year old boy:

I had just concluded a victorious deliverance service in a small church in Illinois. Only the pastor, his family and a few others lingered in the auditorium. The pastor asked, "Brother Frank, would you mind ministering to my little boy, Charles? He really has problems with fear. He is so afraid at night that he pulls the covers over his head, no matter how warm it is. He is also terrified of bugs."

Charles, a five-year-old, was sitting by himself about half way back in the small auditorium, waiting for his parents to take him home. When I took one step toward him, Charles jumped out of his seat and ran as fast as he could out the front door and down the street. The father set in right after him, caught him, and brought the struggling, protesting boy to me.

I said, "Charles, those bad spirits are making you afraid. They even tried to make you run away. Let's tell those spirits to leave, so you won't be afraid any more." The lad began to settle down. The mother had joined us by this time. It was comforting to Charles to have both parents close by.

Next, I addressed the spirits of night-troubling and fear of bugs, and I bound them in the name of Jesus. I told them that they would not be able to make Charles afraid any longer; they were losing their home.

The demons came out with a few sobs. I felt a release in my spirit. Afterward, the pastor and his wife took me to a cafeteria for lunch. Charles was very peaceful; so much so that his parents commented about it. A few weeks later, I received a letter from the pastor reporting that his son was indeed delivered from all his fears. Enclosed was a picture of Charles with a big grin on his face, holding a large, black, beetle between his thumb and index finger!

The fruit of deliverance is love, joy, peace, patience, kindness, goodness, faithfulness, gentleness and self-control, which are the fruit of the Holy Spirit as set forth in Galatians 5:22,23. We often call demons out by saying, "You demons that hate the fruit of the Spirit of love, joy, peace, etc.; come out in the name of Jesus."

Parents will sound like "a resounding gong or a clanging cymbal" I Cor. 13:1, if they try to force their children into a behavior mold that they themselves do not demonstrate. That is when children get defiant and want to say, "So what? How about you?" It doesn't take them long to see the inconsistency between what a parent demands and what he is.

Children are prepared according to the level of their maturity. The deliverance worker need not launch into a deep theological teaching. One does not need to explain to children how it is possible for a Christian to have a demon. The ministry is simple and direct. They truly have child-like faith.

We were invited to minister to an assembly of students at a Christian school. The ages ranged from six to fourteen years. The principal had prepared the students for our coming. Some of the parents were present, and the others had given their consent.

In preparing the students for deliverance we used a simple illustration from Luke 11:24 in which a demon referred to a person's body as "my house". We then compared that scripture with I Cor. 6:19 which declares, "Your body is a *temple* of the Holy Spirit, who is in you, whom you have received from God." (Emphasis ours)

We explained that our bodies are temples where God dwells. Demons want to take over God's temple, make it their house and control what goes on there.

Then, from Luke 19:45 we read that Jesus went into the temple and cast out those who defiled His temple. When the evil things were cast out, the temple could once again be a place of honor and ministry to God. This simple teaching enabled the children to understand the function and purpose of deliverance. We would evict the bad spirits that had taken up residence in God's house.

We remember one girl in particular who received a very powerful deliverance. She was one of the older girls in the group. She put herself into the deliverance with all her heart. Afterward, she testified how the simple teaching had made it very clear to her why she needed deliverance and how it was to be done. This experience exemplifies what we mean when we say that children do not require a deep, theological explanation of deliverance.

Some deliverance ministers choose to deal with children while they are asleep. They lay hands on a child and pray for him quietly while he sleeps. Sometimes the sleep approach is done out of a concern that the child will be frightened. Our experience has determined that children are not frightened by direct, wide-awake ministry. There may be occasions when the Holy Spirit directs the sleep approach, but, personally, we prefer to hit the demons head-on with all eyes open!

There are as many ways to minister to a child as there are children. Each child has his own unique personality; his own feelings; his own capacity to understand. One should keep this truth in mind when ministering to children.

The preparation required for any given child depends upon his maturity level. We have found it helpful to identify each child with a particular age group. Each age group is handled somewhat differently. The groups are divided thus:

> Birth to two years
> Three to six years
> Seven to twelve years
> Teenagers

Let us take each age group separately and consider the different ways and degrees of preparation required.

Birth to Two Years

An infant, too young to comprehend any sort of explanation, obviously requires no instruction. One of us will hold the baby in our arms and love him with tender words and gentle touch.

First, as we begin ministry, we place our hands on the child's head and confess the power of the blood of Jesus over him. The following prayer is given as an example to be used with children of any age:

Heavenly Father, I declare [child's name] is under the covering of the precious blood of Jesus. Just as in Egypt, an Israelite father placed the blood of the lamb upon the door posts of the house, to protect all who were in that house; I, in faith, place this innocent child under the covering of the blood of Jesus through the parents' profession of Jesus as their Savior.

39

Satan has no right to this child, and cannot harm this child in any way, in Jesus' name.

Three to Six Years

We put small children in our laps so as to straddle our laps with their faces toward us. We often hold a child's face in our hands and talk directly into his eyes. We position the child this way for several reasons. First, we can watch the expressions on his face. Demons readily reveal themselves in the countenance of a person, especially in the eyes.

Second, we can also talk directly to the demons and confront them with spiritual authority that Christ has given to us as His disciples.

Third, we want children to be able to see our countenances and see that our faces radiate the love of Jesus. They will see that we are not threats to them. As one's face reflects Jesus, it ministers security to the child.

Children in this age group need an explanation, but don't go into detail or make it complicated. Do not be afraid to tell them about demons. They already know about demons; they have seen them in the cartoons on television and in today's toys.

Let's pretend that we are preparing to cast evil spirits out of a four-year-old girl. Let's call her Mary Jane. This is how we would explain deliverance: "Mary Jane, God says that your body is like a temple, a special house where His Holy Spirit lives. But bad spirits call your body "their house". The Bible says that when a demon is put out of a person he is put out of his 'house'.

"So, your body is a house where evil spirits want to live. Now, if you are in a house and you want to come out, how do you get out?" We then point to her mouth. "Through the door. Where is the door? Your mouth is the door. When I say, 'Demon, you come out of Mary Jane', it will come out through your mouth". Mary

Jane is then instructed to open her mouth and blow out some breath. This initiates an act of her will.

"Now, a demon is a breath, so let us see you blow your breath out. (We show her what we mean by letting our own breath out and blowing through the mouth). Another way you can get him out is to cough him out. (We then practice coughing). That is how demons will come out through your mouth. Your body is God's house, and your mouth is the door to the house.

"How else can a demon come out of you? A house has windows. Your eyes are the windows of your house. Have you ever seen someone climb out of a window? If a demon comes out of you through your eyes, through your windows, you may have tears. So, if you cry and shed tears you will know that a demon is coming out of you through your windows."

Then we tell Mary Jane, "There are two kinds of spirits in the world. Do you know what God's Spirit is called? He is called the Holy Spirit. The devil has lots of spirits. He is not as powerful as God. He is not everywhere as God is, so he has to have many spirits to help him; and these are called demon spirits.

"Now, Mary Jane, we are going to command the bad spirits to come out of you. When we tell them to go, you can help them to leave by breathing them out".

Then, we proceed with the deliverance, and she understands the process. The Holy Spirit helps her to understand it. We also encourage her faith during the deliverance by pointing out why she is crying or coughing.

Seven to Twelve Years

When it comes to this age group, you should consider whether or not a child has been born again. Some children have a conversion experience before age six, although that is not the norm. There is often an opportunity to lead a child to Christ. In any case, it

41

is good to lead each one in a prayer of confession of sin and faith in the Lord Jesus Christ.

It IS important that the parents who bring a child for deliverance have experienced the new birth. This is how the children can have a valid blood covering. Children need a home where they are brought up "in the training and instruction of the Lord" Eph. 6:4.

With children from seven to twelve years of age, we are definitely dealing with the will of the child. Some of them have the sweetest little wills and obediently comply with whatever you request. Others are stubborn and rebellious and do not willingly cooperate with anything you ask of them. Every child has some kind of will, and, when you start dealing with them, you will soon find out what kind of wills they have.

When you reach a point of resistance, you can be sure that you have come across a strong-willed demon, and you must start requiring that child to do certain things; for example, "Sit up straight. Open your mouth. Pray this prayer after me. Take the gum out of your mouth. Tell the demon to go". This procedure demonstrates that they can govern their own wills.

If that boy or girl will not follow any of your instructions, then it is time to say to the parents, "You know your child, and you know how to get him to cooperate. Whatever you do at home to get this child to obey you, do it now. If it is a stern word; if it is the father standing up and reaching for his belt; whatever you do to get his attention, do it. Most of the time you will not have to carry through to the point of discipline, but there are a few times when we have had to resort to that.

Sometimes, you will encounter a stubborn spirit that will cause a child to close his mouth. The demon will press the child's lips tightly together. You will have to battle that spirit until the child is able to open his mouth. In this case, you deal with the child something like this: "I know you want to open you mouth, and I know you cannot because a demon is there that has shut it." A child comprehends this; he really does. You can battle through the stubbornness, and it is usually a great victory when he finally gets the mouth open. The child senses the breakthrough, and you know that you have won.

Teenagers

When you deal with children past twelve years of age, such youths should definitely be born again. Here you are positively dealing with their wills. They have to repent and forgive all who have ever hurt them or harmed them. We usually take even younger children through a prayer of repentance, forgiveness and confession of Christ as Savior. With teenagers there is more and more involvement with the response of their wills and the relationships that they have with their parents, siblings and Jesus.

Just because a child resists deliverance, it does not mean that he does not need it, that he cannot receive it, or, in fact, that he does not want it. His resistance is usually evidence that he needs deliverance; otherwise, he would not oppose it.

It is a marvelous time in the church today for delivering our children out of the hands of the devil. When God restored the ministry of deliverance, adults began to press in for it; they were hurting, and they knew that they needed help. On the contrary, a child does not have the initiative to go to his pastor and say, "Would you help me? I am hurting." We, who are ministers in the body of Christ, along with the parents, must be sensitive to the needs of the children and make sure that they are not overlooked. Deliverance is THE CHILDREN'S BREAD!

4

DELIVERANCE METHODS

There are very few details in scripture concerning methods employed in deliverance. The one method that stands out above all others is the use of spoken authority. Jesus always spoke to demons with authority, and they obeyed Him. He has given His authority to those who believe in Him and has said:

> I have given you authority to trample on snakes and scorpions [demons] and to overcome all the power of the enemy [the devil]; nothing will harm you.
> Luke 10:19, (Brackets ours)

> And these signs will accompany those who believe: In my name they will drive out demons... Mark 16:17

Because so few examples of deliverance methods are found in Scripture, we are left to employ our own methods, as long as such methods are within the framework of scriptural principles. It is imperative that we keep the ministry of deliverance solidly based upon the Word of God.

The methods we share are those that we learned in "the school of the Holy Spirit" while developing skills and expertise in spiritual warfare. It is our hope that others will gain practical knowledge and understanding from the things that we share. In the final analysis, however, each deliverance worker will develop his own methods; those with which he feels comfortable; those that fit his own personality in accordance with the Word of God.

Individual Deliverance

Again, the importance of the blood of Jesus is emphasized. After giving necessary explanations and instructions to parents and children, we employ the weapon of the blood of Jesus. This is no mere ritual of "pleading the blood" over someone, but a precise declaration of what the blood of Jesus is and what it does for those who believe.

The blood of Jesus is *atoning* blood. Atonement signifies "a covering". Sins are covered, and the sinner is not held accountable before God. The devil cannot use forgiven sins against us. Through Christ's atoning work on the cross, the penalty for sin is canceled, and the curse of sin is overcome.

It is *redeeming* blood, literally buying us back from Satan's grasp and paying the price to deliver us from sin and all of its consequences. Christ's blood paid the price for eternal redemption. Christ's blood is *cleansing* blood, purging the conscience of all guilt and giving us boldness to draw near to God's holy presence. The blood of Jesus is *remitting* blood, sending our sins away never to be reckoned with again. Our Savior's blood *justifies* us; by His blood God declares us righteous. The blood of Jesus is *incorruptible* blood, for it has never died. It has never lost its power. It is as alive today as it was the moment it was shed on Calvary. The blood of Jesus is *precious* blood, for its value is great enough to purchase our redemption. Indeed, the importance of the blood of Jesus being used as a *spiritual weapon* cannot be overemphasized.

> For the accuser of our brothers, who accuses them before our God day and night, has been hurled down. *They overcame him by the blood of the Lamb* and by the word of their testimony. Rev. 12:10,11 (Emphasis ours)

The last plague to come upon Egypt was the death of the first born. Provision was made for the Israelites to escape this plague by placing the blood of the Passover lamb upon the door posts of each house. Thus:

> When the Lord goes through the land to strike down the Egyptians, he will see the blood on the top and sides of the doorframe

45

> and will pass over that doorway, and he will
> not permit the destroyer to enter your houses
> and strike you down.   Exod. 12:23

The deliverance minister, acting in behalf of the parents who bring a child for deliverance, has the authority to appeal to the blood of Christ as a covering for that child. The plot and plan of the Destroyer is aborted and his demons are defeated through faith's application of the atoning blood of Christ.

It is our conviction that as soon as a child is conceived, the devil forms a plot and a plan to capture and destroy his life. He assigns a demon, which scripture calls "the strong man", to carry out his scheme. In fact, we have found some adults who are still struggling against a "strong man" that Satan assigned to them in childhood. Satan systematically pursues his scheme until and unless his plot is discovered and demolished by means of deliverance.

We like to begin deliverance by making the following declaration:

> This child [name] is covered with the precious blood
> of Jesus.   Just as the Israelite fathers applied the
> blood of the lamb to the doorposts of their houses,
> we apply the blood of Jesus to the doorposts of this
> child's body, soul and spirit. "Satan, your plot and
> plan has been discovered. We now destroy your
> plot and plan and dismiss the strong man assigned to
> carry out the plot and plan. This child [name] will
> have peace and rest and fulfill God's plan for his life
> with joy and power. Amen!"

It is effective to lay hands on a child's head while you minister to him. The laying of hands on children follows the example of Jesus.

> Then little children were brought to Jesus for
> him to place his hands on them and pray for
> them....When he had placed his hands on
> them, he went on from there.
>   Matt. 19:13, 15

46

It is not out of the question that Jesus ministered deliverance to children on such occasions. The purpose of the laying on of hands is to apply the anointing of the Holy Spirit. It is awesome how an anointed touch causes demons to react. This is evidenced by the child's resistance to the hand on his head. In most instances he will try to move his head away from the hand or reach up to remove the hand from his head. We have heard children complain, "That hurts me" or "That burns my head". We reply, "Yes, demon, we know that it burns you. It is power that you don't have. It is the anointing that destroys your yoke. Loose this child and come out of him, in the name of Jesus."

The next step is to test the will of the child. Everyone has a will. The will is either active or passive or somewhere in between. (With a strong-willed child, his will must be brought into subjection by use of authority and perseverance.) The deliverance minister must be careful not to become emotionally entangled in the will of the child. When you encounter a stubborn child, he will set his will against the ministry. He will not cooperate but will resist you. The child will not willingly sit on your lap or do anything that you suggest.

When obstinacy is encountered, it is important that the deliverance minister not give in to this stubbornness. It must be remembered that you are not only dealing with the flesh of the child, but you are also dealing with demon spirits: spirits of stubbornness, rebellion, self-will, defiance and others. The will of the child is strongly influenced by demon spirits.

These spirits may cause the child to struggle to get off your lap and struggle against your restraint of his flailing arms and legs. He may be screaming, kicking, clawing and biting. This is no time for faintheartedness. You are engaged in spiritual battle

47

with a heap of flesh thrown in, and you must be committed to see the battle through to victory.

If, on the other hand, the child is weak-willed and passive, you may have difficulty getting the deliverance moving. In such cases, the demons themselves are passive; that is their nature. Dealing with any person, child or adult, who is extremely passive presents a deliverance minister with one of his greatest challenges.

The Lord has given us some techniques which have proven effective. Since the evil spirits and the flesh are entwined, it is necessary to deprive the flesh of its normal contentment in order to activate the demons. One simple way to accomplish this is for the minister to take the child from the parent and place him on his own lap. If a mother, for example, is holding her child, passive demons will nestle down, so to speak, in the child's sense of security in mother's arms. With few exceptions, this tactic of taking the child from mother's arms will activate the ministry.

The passive child usually begins to cry, reach for mother with both arms and flex his little fingers, pleading, "Momma, Momma" - meaning, "Take me, Mother! Help me, Mother!"

The mother must not take her child back or even allow the child to touch her. Otherwise, the demon will receive relief and strength. This can be very hard on mother, because mother's natural instinct is to come to the aid of her child. We either scoot our own chair back or ask her to push her chair back and request the mother not to make physical contact with her child which would give the demons support.

Most mothers readily agree that they have had enough of the mother-clinging spirit. They are willing to do whatever it takes to get the demons out. Some mothers think that it might be better if they left the room; but their input is important because they know what is troubling their children. Mothers need to stay

48

in the room and participate in the deliverance. We encourage them to make eye contact with the child and speak encouraging words.

One can expect various reactions from parents, as well as from children. The hand reaching out to mother and the pleas for comfort are manifestations of the demons of insecurity and control. One must discern what is demonic influence and what are the child's legitimate needs.

The warfare that rages will not only disclose certain spirits within the child but can bring things to the surface in the parent and even in the deliverance minister. If the minister is not free of impatience, frustration and anger, such demons will probably surface in him and will, more than likely, ruin the ministry. **NEVER, NEVER exhibit frustration, impatience or anger** when wrestling with demons in children (or anyone else). The minister must keep his composure at all times. His composure builds security and love ties between himself and the child. Calm assurance speaks peace to the child in the midst of the storm, whereas anger and impatience minister fear.

Demons are masters at stirring up frustration, impatience and anger in parents on a daily basis. An obvious goal of demons is to initiate conflicts between parents and children so as to destroy the joy, peace and worth of their relationship. Deliverance should focus on what Satan has been doing. Put the blame where it belongs, and destroy the devil's works.

Once the deliverance battle has begun, stay committed until the spirits are out and peace prevails. **It is vital to success that you persevere in battle until victory is won.** Oftentimes there will be a lull in the battle, but the battle will not be over. It is a mistake to quit too soon. As long as the child continues to struggle, the ministry is incomplete. If, because of weariness or intimidation, the ministry is terminated prematurely, the value of the ministry is lost.

When demons get loud and noisy, there is a temptation for the deliverance minister to get loud and noisy. One never needs to yell at demons in either children or adults in order to cast them out. The key to casting out demons is in using **spiritual authority**.

Authority can be spoken in a whisper. Try putting your mouth right next to the ear of the child and whisper, "I tell you, demon, leave in the name of Jesus. I put my foot on your neck, and I rule over you in Jesus' name." Depend upon The Holy Spirit to give you specific words to speak. Words of spiritual authority put pressure on the demons which weakens and drives them out.

Demons cause enough furor without our creating a furor, too. Keep on pressing the spirits, and pressure them with the name of Jesus until they come out. The Bible calls this kind of warfare, "wrestling" Ephesians 6:12. Demons are not always cast out with a single command. Even Jesus drove out demons with repeated commands.[13] Continue to speak the name of Jesus and proclaim the power of His blood to redeem, atone, justify and cleanse. Keep on telling the demons that they must go in the name of Jesus, until they are gone. It is not unusual for the warfare to last thirty minutes or longer.

Ida Mae recalls a ministry that illustrates several of the points that have just been made.

I was ministering to a little girl about seven or eight
years old. It was a group deliverance situation in a
large church, and the little girl was sitting on the

---

[13]In Mark, 5:8, AMPLIFIED BIBLE, "Jesus was commanding (progressive action verb), Come out of the man, you unclean spirit!" In Matthew 8:16, Jesus "drove out spirits with *a* word". The article "a" is supplied to render a smooth translation. Literally, He "drove out spirits with word", that is, with spoken authority.

front row with her mother. She wasn't cooperating with the ministry at all. She was sitting there with lips pouted and arms folded across her chest, and there she sat.

I asked the little girl to come sit with me. I took her by the arm, lifted her out of her chair and drew her into my lap. Right away I knew we were in for some strenuous warfare because of the nature of the demons controlling her.

With the mother sitting in front of me, I went through all of my usual procedures: covering her with the blood, and its anointing power, and warring against the spirits. Absolutely nothing happened. The girl still had her mouth clamped shut with her lips in a pout.

I asked the mother to help, and I gave the instructions in such a way that the girl herself would hear and understand. I said, "Mother, these demons have this child's mouth shut, and they are very strong demons. I want you to tell her to open her mouth, and I want you to use your fingers to gently pry her mouth open. This will break up this stalemate and activate her will enough for her to get her mouth open; then we can start getting the spirits out."

I kept instructing over and over for her to open her mouth, for the Holy Spirit had given me a word of knowledge that her fleshly will had to be dealt with. Her own will was in agreement with strong-willed demons, but once that she, of her own will, opened her mouth the hindrance to the deliverance would be removed.

The mother kept trying to get her to open her mouth while I kept warring the spirits. The warring went something like this: "Now demons, while we are working to get her to open her mouth, I will strip you of your power. You have no more right to control her because her mother and father have agreed you must leave their daughter. All your legal rights have been broken. The blood of Jesus sets her free. The name of Jesus gives me authority over you. Loose your control! I strip you of all your strength You are powerless before me, in Jesus' name. By the anointing I am getting stronger, but you are getting weaker. Lose your power now!"

The mother would press on the daughter's chin and tell her to open her mouth. Finally, the mother got the daughter's mouth open enough to get her thumb in between her teeth, and we kept up this procedure for about five minutes. That may not sound like a long time, but it seemed a long time to us.

Tears began to well up in the little girl's eyes. This was a welcome sign to me, for I knew it was an indication that the demons were admitting defeat. I explained to her that if she would only open her mouth the demons would come out.

More tears began to come, and I knew that the stubborn spirits were being affected. As we kept up the pressure on the spirits, I encouraged the girl to cough, as another act of her will, hoping that the spirits would come out that way. Finally, she began to sob. I encouraged her, explaining that the demons were dissolving into water and coming out. At that point we had to take her into a back room to finish her deliverance because the group deliverance had finished, and we were interfering with the general service.

At last, her own will was beginning to cooperate; for, when I asked her to go with us, she hopped down from my lap and went with us into the back room. I said, "If you, will help us we can finish your deliverance in a few minutes. We want you to help us. You are going to feel better when we get these bad spirits out."

We picked up right where we had left off, and I said, "In the name of Jesus", and that little girl let out a piercing scream. I said, "That's all right; do anything you want to do to get them out. Stomp your foot or do anything else you feel like doing to get them out." I repeated, "In the name of Jesus come out of her", and she clenched her fists and screamed and screamed.

A lot of flesh was in her actions, but that was all right, she was no longer passive or stubborn; she was doing something! She screamed about six times, and it was all over. That was the end.

The mother and I both had assurance in our spirits that the battle had been won. I began to edify the little girl by bragging about how hard she fought and how well she did. I kept saying, "You are a good girl. You did that so well. I'm proud of you."

I visited with the mother the next day, and she told me that there was a big difference in her little girl. She explained the pattern of behavior that had been in her daughter. After she got up each morning she would not speak to anyone. She remained silent half the morning. If someone said, "Good morning", she would not respond. "What do you want for breakfast?" She wouldn't answer; still in complete silence. The morning would be half gone before she ever said one word. Mother now reported, "This morning she bounded into church speaking to everyone."

I want to convey to everyone that it is important to understand the nature of a child. It helps to provoke the flesh when dealing with spirits in a passive child. I do not imply that one should get rough with a child. **Never, never** abuse a child in any sense of the word. While dealing sternly with demons, you must deal lovingly and fairly with the child.

The Lord will give little techniques to get a ministry going, and it is really exciting when He shows you what to do.

I am not opposed to a parent spanking his child if he refuses to cooperate, and if the child is old enough to know right from wrong. God's Word recommends spanking as a means of child discipline. "Folly[14] is bound up in the heart of a child, but the rod of discipline will drive it far from him" Prov. 22:1.

If self-will, stubbornness and rebellion keep a child from receiving deliverance, then the devil has won the day. We leave it up to the parents to obtain a child's cooperation. We encourage parents to use whatever means of parental authority they deem wise to obtain obedience and cooperation. The flesh *does* require discipline. Sometimes one must let a child know that he is not in control but that you are in control. In order for children to get deliverance, we must get past stubborn and passive flesh that sometimes stands in the way.

In another situation, in Europe, it was a father who was unable to be a disciplinarian. His eight-year-old daughter was very stubborn and self-willed, refusing to comply to the simplest request. I had asked her to sit in a certain chair, but she refused. I finally had to take her by the arm and move her to the chair. I explained to her that demons were in her tummy and would come out through her mouth with her breath.

(Let me insert here that I have never seen a child exhibit fear when I spoke about demons being in his or her tummy. Children have a sweet, simple faith, and they never stumble over the issue of indwelling spirits. Interestingly, it is only adults who ever show fear or

---

[14]The Hebrew word *ivveleth*, translated "folly", refers to "one who acts without counsel and whose will is too hard for his understanding". Wilson, Old Testament Word Studies, Kregel Publication, 1978, p. 172.

disbelief over the idea that they can have demons inside them.)

I then asked the girl to open her mouth and blow out her breath. I was not surprised when she refused. The Holy Spirit gave me a word of knowledge that I was not to proceed any further until she complied.

I continued with persuasion although I was sure it wouldn't work. At the same time I was waiting for the Holy Spirit's direction.

The mother observed the proceedings as she remained seated with folded arms. Finally she commented, "See what I have to put up with? This is why we are here." I then became aware that the father was totally detached and aloof. I said to myself, "Ah, ha! There's the problem." I turned to the father and asked, "Can you get her to respond?" The mother readily spoke up, "That is our other problem." The father was obviously uncomfortable when the attention shifted to him.

A little conversation brought out the key to resolving the dilemma. This father felt that his own father's discipline had been unfair, harsh and abusive, which built anger in himself. Out of concern that his anger might cause him to abuse his own children, he withdrew from his rightful position as the head of his family, and left all discipline to his wife. He salved his conscience by working hard, making money and giving them everything they needed *except* fatherly attention and caring enough to discipline.

I had him read Hebrews 12:5, 6: "My son, do not regard lightly the discipline of the Lord. Nor faint when you are reproved by Him; *For those whom the Lord loves He disciplines*, and He scourges every son whom He receives."

I pointed out to him that he had become faint-hearted because of his own father's harsh discipline. Now, his reluctance to discipline had put an unfair hardship on his wife and alienated himself from his daughter. Her deepest need was to know that Dad loved her enough to correct and discipline her.

I bound the spirit of fear, and asked the Holy Spirit to give him inner strength to resolve our dilemma. Perspiration broke out on his forehead and upper lip. It was as though he had been glued to his seat; then, suddenly and forcefully he stood up. That was all he did; he just stood to his feet.

Immediately, the daughter opened her mouth and was breathing in and out so fast and hard that she almost hyperventilated.   I simultaneously started calling out the spirits, and the deliverance began. I was awed and elated, for I was seeing Satan's kingdom demolished before my very eyes.

Afterward, I encouraged the mother to back off on the discipline and let her husband learn to bear that responsibility. She assured me that this would be no problem for her.   Then we all had a good laugh together. We were all so relieved and overjoyed at the victory God had brought about.

Discipline is a way of ministering love and giving needed attention. Children who are deprived of love and attention will often develop bad behavior because they are trying to force parents to notice them.   It comes across as rejection when children are deprived of needed discipline. Spanking and other forms of correction show that parents care.

Ida Mae recalls a specific situation where a mother spanked a daughter to gain the child's cooperation for deliverance. Several valuable truths are brought to light in the following account:

A father and mother brought their two daughters, ages eight and nine, for deliverance. When they arrived, the mother reported having heard the older girl tell her younger sister that they would not cooperate. This was a pattern of behavior with the two girls. The older girl would tell her sister what to do.   The younger girl just watched the older one, and she did whatever her sister did or whatever she told her to do.

We were in a family camp, and the children were scheduled to be in a special activity at the only time we could give them an appointment. This change in plans had made them both unhappy. Sure enough, they would not do anything that we asked them to do. Frank, the father and I each encouraged, persuaded, and did everything we could; but nothing was happening. The older girl would look at her sister, and it was apparent that both were agreed on total non-cooperation.

Whereas the father was gentle but firm with the girls, I became aware that the mother seemed rather detached and very uninvolved with the situation. None of my techniques were working, and I was getting frustrated. The father suddenly had to leave to meet an appointment. At the moment I felt that this was most unfortunate, but I was soon to discover that God was working all things together for good.

I prayed, "Lord, what do I do to get this going?" He spoke to my spirit, "The mother needs to spank the older one." I told the mother that she should take the oldest girl into the bathroom and spank her. The mother said, "I can't do that. I've never been able to do that". The mother was reluctant to discipline the girls because she had been disciplined harshly and unfairly as a child, and she was fearful that she would be abusive if she spanked her daughters. She could not bring herself to spank the children, so the burden of all discipline was on the father.

The Lord had a twofold plan: the child needed discipline, and the mother needed to overcome her inability to minister discipline. We gave the mother a quick teaching on discipline, and suggested that she take the older girl into the bathroom and give her a spanking. The mother tried to excuse herself further: "I can't do that," she said, "I don't have a paddle." The

Lord called my attention to the fact that the mother was wearing flat-bottomed shoes, so I suggested that she use a shoe for a paddle. So, she pulled off her shoe, took the girl into the bathroom, and gave her daughter about three good swats.

While the mother was giving the older girl a spanking, I said to her sister, "You are next, unless you decide to cooperate with the deliverance." Instantly she started coughing and gagging, coughing and gagging as the demons came rolling out. She got a good deliverance. Then the older girl, with a remarkable attitude change, returned to the room with her mother. Frank sat the older girl on his lap, and she cooperated fully and received a good deliverance.

The deliverance for the older girl defeated the control spirit which was truly making a non-person out of the younger sister. We could discern the demon of *control of sister* melting away!

"Hey, kids", I exclaimed, "Mom is next!" Then I said, "Mother, it is your turn; you need some deliverance." The kids loved seeing their mother being prayed for just as they had been. They joined in with me, and we prayed for Mom. She needed deliverance from spirits which kept her from taking initiative with her children. She had never been able to discipline or control them.

The above account illustrates how an entire family oftentimes needs deliverance together. There are spirits which intertwine and work in conjunction with one another within a household. Spirits in one member of a family interplay with spirits in others.

A few weeks later, the parents of the two girls wrote us a follow-up report on the ministry. After they left camp, they had taken the girls to a Six Flags fun park. All the former conflicts were gone. The girls' relationship was greatly improved, and their attitudes were different. It was the best time they had ever had together as a family.

Spanking a child in order to gain cooperation is a last resort. This was the only time I can recall when I asked a parent to spank a child. Remember, I was acting on a special word of knowledge given for this specific occasion.

Deliverance ministers have been known to fall into the deception of making a doctrine out of a successful experience. One can easily reason, "I ministered in a certain way, and I got a good result, so I will minister the same way every time." No, we must remain open to the leading of the Holy Spirit in every given situation.

A few people are critical of the methods that we follow in ministering deliverance. These have advised, "Just speak the word in faith, brother, and believe that all the demons have gone." Faith is indeed essential in ministering deliverance. Demons know whether or not the worker has faith, but faith works in conjunction with supernatural words of knowledge and wisdom. Parents must gain an understanding of how demons were allowed to enter their children, and they need to understand the nature of the demons. Otherwise, parents will not know how to keep those same demons from returning. Parents often need to make corrections in their own lives as well as to foster changes in the lives of their children.

Be patient and merciful with children. Above all, minister in love. One must love children, love deliverance ministry and love Jesus in order to minister properly to children, or to anyone, for that matter. Children know whether or not you love them. They can be acting like tigers, but they know whether you love them, and genuine love is hard to ignore.

Most of the time, when ministering to very small children, I call out vexing, tormenting and troubling spirits. The Syrophonecian woman who sought deliverance for her little daughter said, "My daughter is grievously *vexed* with a devil" Matt. 15:22, KJ. The word "vexed" means disturbed, troubled, harassed and distressed. This describes children who fret, cry and are irritable. Nothing pacifies this child. He is vexed. So, I call out vexing spirits.

Of course, the child may be cutting teeth, so one must have some common sense. It is important that you utilize the gift of discerning of spirits when ministering to children.

There are occasions when you will call out a whole nest of demons at one time, rather than casting them out one by one. A child may be labeled "a problem child". This being true, a whole nest of demons can be cast out by commanding the "problem child" demons to go from him. These demons torment the mother and wreck her nerves.

"Problem child" is a very bad confession to make over one's son or daughter. Children will become and remain whatever is spoken over them. "The tongue has the power of life and death" Prov. 18:21. Children can be put under the power of a demonic curse by being labeled with negative confessions. Some parents say to others in the presence of the child, "This is my problem child. I can't do anything with him." We admonish parents to change their confession and speak positive words of praise and blessing over their children.

When the warfare phase of ministry is complete, it is not unusual for a small child to go to sleep or lie motionless and relaxed in your arms. However, this does not terminate the ministry. **Do not rush the ending!** Always spend time loving the child and ministering Jesus to him. It is time to glorify and exalt God with praise and thanksgiving for what He has done.

Make positive confessions; speak peace, joy, acceptance, righteousness and fruitfulness into his life. Announce to the devil that his evil plan for this child has been cast to the ground, and defeated and acknowledge that Jesus' plan for his life will be fulfilled. Declare that this child has been brought forth to usher in Jesus Christ, the Anointed One and the King of Kings, and that he will never serve the Antichrist. Expect the Lord to give you a personal word for each child, something that is directly from Him.

Group Deliverance
Throughout His earthly sojourn Jesus ministered to multitudes of people, many of whom were demonized.

> People brought to him all who were ill with various diseases, those suffering severe pain, the demon- possessed, the epileptics and the paralytics, and he healed them. Large crowds from Galilee, the Decapolis, Jerusalem, Judea and the region across the Jordan followed him.   Matt. 4:24-25

> When evening came, many who were demon-possessed were brought to him, and he drove out the spirits with a word and healed all the sick.   Matt. 8:16

How was Jesus able to minister to so many? We can assume that He did not spend two hours with each person in counsel and individual ministry. There is no logical explanation other than that He ministered to the people as a group by the power of His anointing. We know this is possible, for we have participated in both mass healing and deliverance services with powerful anointing of the Holy Spirit.

As we began to travel and minister to large gatherings of people, we found it imperative to minister to them *en masse*. The Lord not only taught us that this is possible, but He blessed us with a greater anointing. The following is the procedure that the Lord gave us for group deliverance for children:

First, we announce the meeting several days in advance. We normally have the special time for children on the third or fourth day of a conference.

61

This gives us an opportunity to minister to the parents first. It is best for parents to have deliverance before their children for two reasons: They set a good example for the children, and they become free enough to help with their children's ministry.

Second, we instruct the parents to accompany their children. As we have already emphasized, parents are the spiritual guardians and providers for their sons and daughters. Parents need to know what spirits are cast out, and we want them to participate in the actual deliverance. We also make it clear that they are not to bring neighborhood children, even though they are obviously filled with demons. It is important to have parents or guardians who will be responsible for follow-up ministry and protect their children from demonic attacks. Whenever possible, we prefer to have both father and mother present. God has charged fathers with the spiritual oversight of the family. We regularly experience more effective ministry when the father is present.

Third, families are asked to sit together. In some meeting places we can arrange their chairs in a circle. If there is extra space in the auditorium; it is best to have everyone spread out, in order that each family can have at least a semi-private setting.

Fourth, there is a short time for teaching and instructions. We keep in mind that small children have short attention spans, and they cannot be expected to sit still for long periods of time. The instructions are primarily for the parents.

Our teaching starts with one of us reading the Gospel account where Jesus ministered to the Syrophonecian woman's little daughter.[15] Next, we read about the nobleman's seriously demon-oppressed son whom Jesus gloriously delivered.[16] From these

---

[15]Mark 7:24-30.
[16]Luke 9:37-42

Scriptures we draw out principles of deliverance and show how Jesus Himself cast demons out of children.

It is also appropriate to point out that deliverance is not an instant cure for all childhood problems. Deliverance is not a substitute for a stable home environment; proper teaching and training; proper and consistent correction; protection from harmful influences, and abundant amounts of consistent love.

The practical instructions include a reminder that parents will minister directly to their children under our directions. Fathers and mothers are instructed to lay hands on their children's heads or tummies and command the spirits to come out.

Parents must help passive children to participate and require rebellious children to cooperate. Cooperation includes getting rid of chewing gum, expelling one's breath when instructed, sitting up straight, staying awake and not creating distractions.

Parents are coached to watch for reactions after deliverance begins. For example, demons cause some children to react strongly when hands are placed on their heads. Small children are sometimes prone to bite, kick and scratch. Some clamp their mouths shut. Others manifest anger, rebellion, defiance, stubbornness or self-consciousness. There may be crying or sulking. Some get very sleepy. Small children often nestle down in the parent's arms, which provides an opportunity for their demons to nestle down, also.

Fifth, we spend a few minutes talking directly to the children to put them at ease and gain their cooperation. We ask special questions for them to answer: Have you been born again? How many of you are baptized in the Holy Spirit? Have you ever told a lie? Stolen? What are you most afraid of? (Dogs, the dark, strangers, punishment, etc.) Can you give me an example of a good spirit? (An angel or the

Holy Spirit). Give an example of a bad spirit. (A demon).

We use the analogy from Scripture of demons calling a person's body his "house" and explain that houses have doors and windows. The mouth is the "door" of the "body house" and eyes are the "windows". We clarify how demons come out through the mouth with yawns, coughs, burps, cries and sighs, or they sometimes come out through the eyes with tears.

Sixth, we lead the group in prayer. For example: "Father in Heaven, we thank You for this time to honor our children. We ask You to touch each one and deliver them from every oppression of the enemy. We know that You love each one of these precious children, for You gave Jesus to die on the cross to be their Savior".

"Lord, we cover each one with the precious blood of Jesus. Just as the Israelite fathers placed the blood of the lamb upon the door posts of the houses to protect everyone in the house, we, by faith, place the atoning blood of Jesus, the perfect Lamb of God, upon the door posts of each heart".

"In the name of Jesus we declare the destruction of the plot and plan that Satan has devised for each child. In the name of Jesus we bind every spirit that would try to rob us of what God has provided". "Satan, we forbid you to hinder, distract, confuse or in any way interfere with this time of deliverance. You are bound and your house is spoiled. We take back all that you have ever stolen. In Jesus' name. Amen."

We then invite the Holy Spirit to release the anointing for deliverance. When the anointing comes, the evil spirits are put under pressure, which causes restlessness and crying among the children.

Seventh, we cast out demons which are common to children.[17] As we go through this list, commanding the

---

[17]See: Listing of demons common to children in Chapter 6.

64

demons to go, we listen carefully with our spiritual ears for special words of knowledge and discerning of spirits. The Holy Spirit usually gives us the names of other demons to be cast out.

Parents are told not to slavishly follow the order of demons that are called out by us from the pulpit. They are encouraged to focus on the personal needs of their own children. Before the time of deliverance ends, we give parents an opportunity to challenge whatever spirits that still concerned them. We have discovered that in group deliverance sessions there is usually a strong anointing for corporate deliverance. Individuals will receive much more liberation than initially might be recognized.

Finally, we instruct the parents to lay hands on their children and bless them, following the example of Jesus. "And he (Jesus) took the children in his arms, put his hands on them and blessed them" Mark 10:16. We tell the children they are loved and express appreciation for their cooperation.

It is beneficial to have counselors to help when deliverance is ministered to groups. These counselors are instructed to move about the room assisting those who need special or extra assistance. They are encouraged to minister in the anointing of the Holy Spirit, functioning in the gifts of the Spirit.

It is not unusual for persons experiencing deliverance to drool, cough up phlegm, have runny noses and weep. So, as a practical matter, we instruct our counselors to have a handful of facial tissues or paper towels to dispense to those who need them.

We are confident in saying that some of the most anointed times of deliverance that we have experienced are the children's group ministries. It is evident that our Lord loves children and youth and provides the best for them.

Through their participation in group ministry, parents learn how readily they can minister to their own children at home. They discover how to go about it and gain confidence to do it themselves. They are thereby released from dependence upon some "expert" deliverance minister to come along or from having to wait for another children's deliverance session.

5

DEMONIC MANIFESTATIONS

What is meant by "demon manifestation"? "Manifest" means to make a show or display so that something is readily perceived by the senses, especially by sight. When a demons manifests within a person, they display their presence and revea their nature through controlling the faculties of the one they indwell. The account of the Gadarene demoniac is an example. Demons influenced this wretched fellow to dwell in a cemetery, gave him supernatural strength, caused him to cry out day and night and to cut himself with stones. Further, they spoke through the man's voice and begged Jesus to allow them to go into a herd of swine (Mark 5:5, 11).

What kind of manifestations can one expect when ministering to children? We have experienced a wide range of manifestations: yawning, burping, coughing, crying, mocking, demons speaking, phlegm, supernatural strength, flailing, hitting, biting, clawing, wetting and others.

While ministering deliverance to an eight year old girl, she started laughing. The mother became very angry with the girl and said, "What do you mean by laughing?" Ida Mae said, "That's all right. It's the demon laughing; just let him laugh. It is a mocking spirit. She probably laughs at you inwardly when you discipline her. He is going to come out." Ida then said to the demon, "That's all right demon; you may laugh now, but we are going to have the last laugh!"

The laughing continued for awhile and then the girl began to cry. This was followed by other manifestations. So, you can expect all sorts of manifestations to occur. The most common manifestation is crying: a lot of crying. However, you cannot presuppose what manifestations will occur.

We were ministering to a family that had four little girls. We started with the infant, who was about three-months-old. During her deliverance there was a great deal of crying. Next, we ministered to the three-year-old. Again, there was much crying. When we came to the next child, the father said, "I don't know whether or not I have strength for this one. The first two are good kids, but the one you are about to minister to is terrible. If the good kids acted like that, I don't know whether or not I have the strength for this onet." Ida Mae said, "We will have the strength; the Lord will see to that."

We challenged the spirits in the girl, and she was a yawner. She just yawned and yawned and yawned. So, the one whose behavior was the worst had the mildest manifestations. Afterward, we all had a good laugh about it.

We cannot predict what type of manifestations any given person will have, and we have no explanation for the seeming contradiction of violent spirits coming out with yawns.

The important thing to look for is the fruit of deliverance, not manifestations. This "terrible" little girl who yawned out the spirits, afterward, had the fruit of deliverance in her life. After being prayed for, she experienced changes in her behavior and attitude.

When working with very young children, there are two manifestations that are quite common. First, is the wringing of the hands and/or rubbing the feet together. Second, is their reaching out toward mother and begging for sympathy. This really melts a mother's heart. Instinctively, she will reach out to take the child, but we say, "No, do not touch him, because that gives the demons strength. Sit there and have eye contact, give words of encouragement, but do not touch him."

The kind and degree of manifestations do not necessarily indicate the validity or degree of the deliverance attained. Some slight or imperceptible manifestations sometimes accompany great deliverance. Manifestations can give a sense of confidence to ministers and parents, but manifestations must not become the criteria for judging the success of the ministry.

Faith is the key to dislodging demons. A seasoned deliverance minister should not have to have manifestations to build his faith. The Bible says we are not moved by what we see but by faith in the Word of God. But manifestations often help to sustain faith in those receiving and observing deliverance.

Demons do not manifest for the benefit of the deliverance minister, or others present, but because of the pressure of losing their "house"; as they are brought out of darkness into light. All of the armor in which they trust is being taken away. An evil spirit's strongest defense is the darkness created by deception.

Deliverance draws demons out of darkness and exposes them to the light of truth; therefore, frenzied manifestations occur. Any creature, whether animal, bird or insect, whose habitat is darkness is made restless and agitated when exposed to light. Demons are no different.

Sometimes evil spirits manifest in an attempt to confuse us or divert our attention from something important. By way of illustration, a dove will protect her young by pretending to be crippled, drawing the predator or hunter away from her nest. Demons likewise use distracting tactics such as bizarre manifestations to distract the deliverance minister from his intended mission. Be careful not to follow the manifestation instead of following the Holy Spirit, or you will be fooled as is the predator by the play-acting bird, and you will miss your quarry. The gift of wisdom enables you to be wiser than they: to rule over them rather than they over you.

One should not encourage demons to speak through a person, for this de-edifies that person and exalts pride in the minister. A deliverance minister can cultivate a demon circus, if he so wishes, by encouraging demons to manifest. We have seen a few instances when the deliverance minister would find a person in the audience who was manifesting readily and bring that person to the front for all to observe. It is our conviction that such tactics dishonor the person and also the Lord.

Jesus never permitted demons to bear witness. When a demon blurted out, "I know thee who thou art, the Holy one of God...Jesus rebuked him, saying, Hold thy peace, and come out of him" Mark 1:24,25. Allowing demons to talk by encouraging them to talk may produce an unwarranted awe of the devil.

Demons are no dummies. They know the character of the deliverance minister, and if he is a person given to pride, the demons will play up to his pride and draw him into a snare. When Jesus sent his disciples out to minister, he counseled them, "Be as wise as serpents and as harmless as doves" Matt. 10:16.

There is a difference between ministering deliverance to children and ministering to adults. When Jesus ministered to children He, "Took them in His arms and laid His hands on them" Mark 10:16. Likewise we take them in our arms and hold them because they are not mature enough physically and spiritually to resist the devil and yield to God. They follow natural inclinations and allow the nature of demons to manifest.

Demons convey or betray their basic natures by their types of manifestations. For example: a mocking spirit will cause the child to laugh; a stubborn spirit will shut his mouth; a deceiving spirit will say, "You're hurting me" or "I need the bathroom" or "a drink of water". Distracting spirits sometimes cause the child the ask questions, such as, "Why are you holding me?"

When a deliverance minister doubts or fears that nothing will happen, he is tempted to do something on his own and thereby act in the flesh or even rely upon demons to tell him what to do. (This should remind us of King Saul, who, when Samuel, the king's spiritual counselor, died; and the Philistines had pitched their army against Israel, Saul "was afraid" and sought counsel of the Witch of Endor).[18] As a consequence, the Philistines prevailed in the battle and the Lord rent the kingdom out of Saul's hands. Therefore, we see that it is a serious matter to attempt deliverance without the guidance and power of the Holy Spirit.

---

[18]See: I Sam. 28:3-18

6
DEMONS COMMON TO CHILDREN

When ministering deliverance to a child, the minister should be as thorough as possible. It is helpful to keep in mind that demons establish themselves in an individual's life in a systematic and organized way. In every situation, one is literally dealing with a network of spirits which has a "strong man" in charge. A ruler spirit is at the root of the problem.

Within a network of evil spirits, groups or families of spirits are found. Birds of a feather flock together, and, in the same way, demons of like nature work together in tenacious cooperation. Jesus pointed out that Satan's kingdom is not divided (Matt. 12:25,26); therefore, it is no surprise that there is cooperation and unity with evil intent within his ranks.

Jesus taught that deliverance is carried out by first entering the strong man's house [his dwelling place] and binding the strong man [neutralizing his power]; then, spoiling his household [reversing whatever problems the inhabiting demons have caused]. See: Matt. 12:29[19].

How can a parent or deliverance minister determine what demons need to be cast out? Spirits can be detected by simply observing the child. What obvious problem is the child manifesting? Is he hyperactive, uncooperative, rebellious, withdrawn, insecure, irritable, unhappy or passive?

Demons can also be detected by questioning the parents. For, example, does he have learning problems, chronic sickness or specific fears? What

---

[19]In Matt. 12:29, the Greek word *oikia*, means house, household or family.

nationalities are in the family background? Has there been occult involvement, false religious practices, addictions or sexual transgressions in the known family background? Have there been any trauma experiences (direct or indirect), such as: severe illness, accidents, abandonment, deaths (relatives, friends or pets), or abuse?

There are some things that open doors to demons that one would never discover through the avenues of human understanding; therefore, one must go beyond observation and inquiry. One must rely upon the Holy Spirit for supernatural words of knowledge, words of wisdom, and discerning of spirits and the gift of faith.

> Now to each one the manifestation of the Spirit is given for the common good. To one there is given through the Spirit the message of wisdom, to another the message of knowledge by means of the same Spirit, to another faith by the same Spirit...to another the ability to distinguish between spirits...All these are the work of the one and the same Spirit, and he gives them to each man, just as he determines.   I Cor. 12:7-11

Wisdom, knowledge, faith and discerning of spirits are gifts of the Holy Spirit, and all deliverance ministers should "eagerly desire spiritual gifts" I Cor. 14:1. The gift of faith gives assurance that the "mountain" in a child's life will be removed. The gift of faith also provides boldness and courage to initiate the ministry. Other gifts of the Holy Spirit direct the minister in how to begin, how to continue and how to complete the deliverance warfare.

A list of demons common to children would be incomplete without some accompanying commentary. First, for organization and clarification sake, let us examine the following categories of spirits commonly encountered in deliverance with children and youth. After that, we will list demons which we commonly encounter in children's deliverances.

Inherited Curses

Most children are born with spirits of inherited curses. The law of God states that curses pass down to succeeding generations due to the iniquities of the fathers.

> I, the Lord your God, am a jealous God, punishing the children for the sin of the fathers to the third and fourth generations of those who hate me.   Exod. 20:5

Curses are set in motion when God's hand of blessing is removed, and demons are allowed to attack. Demons are the power source accompanying curses. When there are unresolved sins in the family background, demons have a legal right to indwell the descendants of those who have transgressed God's laws.

The power to reverse the curse of the law is found in the Cross:

> Christ redeemed us from the curse of the law by becoming a curse for us, for it is written: "Cursed is everyone who is hung on a tree."
> Gal. 3:13

One must appropriate by faith the provisions of the Cross: forgiveness of sins and authority over demons. Therefore, let the sins of the forefathers be confessed and forsaken.   Then, cast out the demons sent to perpetuate the curse.

Identifying Inherited Curses

Inherited curses can be identified either by observing or discerning family sins or by noting the problems that curses cause.   We recommend a thorough study of two chapters in the Old Testament which are devoted to blessings and curses. Deuteronomy, chapter twenty-seven, lists the basic causes for curses, and chapter twenty-eight forcefully presents the effects of curses.[20]

---

[20]For a fuller treatment on "Curses", see: *The Breaking Of*

74

For example, inherited curses are found to be caused by the sins of idolatry; occult practices; dishonoring parents; sexual sins (fornication, adultery, incest, bestiality, homosexuality and all other perversions); fraud; injustice toward widows, orphans, strangers and the handicapped; unethical business practices; illegitimacy; murder (including abortion and suicide) and all other transgressions of God's law.

The effects of inherited curses include sickness, poverty, insanity, blindness, defeat, fear, life traumas (unfaithfulness of one's spouse, loss of property, business failures, barrenness, divorce, destruction and death.)

Channels Which Inherited Curses Follow

Curses are passed down from generation to generation through home environment. Children are adversely affected by wrong examples set before them: alcohol, tobacco, drugs, illicit sex, disrespect, quarreling, fighting, abuse, lying and stealing. These sorts of problems are regularly perpetuated, and sometimes intensified, in succeeding generations.

Take, for example, the case of Abraham's lying about Sarah being his wife. On two different occasions, he lied by saying that Sarah was his sister. He lied out of fear to save his own skin. Yet, what he said was a half-truth, for Sarah was actually his half-sister.

Abraham's son, Isaac, followed in his father's footsteps by telling the same lie about his wife, Rebecca. Isaac's was an out-and-out lie. Thus, the sin of lying was passed down through direct influence of one generation upon the next. If it had not been for the sovereign intervention of God, both Sarah and Rebecca would have been in serious trouble. Notwithstanding,

---

Curses by F. & I.M. Hammond, Impact Christian Books, Inc., 1993.

as sinful influences pass down from generation to generation, corresponding curses are perpetuated.

Genes, chromosomes and blood are other channels utilized by inherited curses. It is advisable to cleanse these channels through which inherited curses move. Simply, command out all spirits that have entered through these avenues.

Prenatal Influences

Life begins at the point of conception. We are fully persuaded of this fact through our experience in ministering deliverance to embryos and fetuses in the wombs of expectant mothers. These are living organisms, human beings: not mere blobs of tissue. Demons take notice of every conception, and immediately devise their plans of attack.

Demons seek to indwell living beings, especially those through which they can carry out their evil agenda. Their preference of human life above animal life is exemplified in the case of the Gadarene demoniac. When Legion, a ruler spirit over thousands of lesser demons, was cast out, all the demons begged Jesus' permission to enter a herd of swine. The pigs were their second choice.

Destruction and death were the ultimate goals of the demons, as evidenced in the entire herd of swine rushing over a cliff and being drowned in the sea. Likewise, destruction and death are the ultimate goals of demons who find an opening into an unborn baby. Demons are evil spirits whose aims coincide with their father, the devil. "He was a murderer from the beginning" John 8:44. Surely, abortion must give demons special satisfaction.

We have ministered to numbers of people who have been involved in abortions in one way or another - the pregnant woman, the father of the aborted baby, the abortionist and his staff, the pro-choicer - and each of them, without exception, needed deliverance from spirits of murder.[21]

A spirit of death gains a legal right to a child yet in the womb if the mother and/or father attempt or even contemplate an abortion. Spirits of rejection can enter if, for any reason, the pregnancy is unwanted. Since a mother and the baby in her womb are so closely linked together, the mother's emotions and physical activities directly affect the baby, even in its embryonic state. Therefore, a baby can be born with fears and insecurities thorough the unstable emotions of the mother.

Addictive drugs used by the mother pass right through the placenta into the baby. The baby may suffer physical problems and come into the world addicted to nicotine, alcohol, cocaine or other addictive substances (both medically prescribed and illegal). Immediately after birth, some babies go through painful withdrawal from drugs.

When the mother is given the drug patosium to induce labor, this drug passes through the placenta into the baby affecting the nervous system with adverse effects upon his emotions. We routinely cover this in children's deliverance situations when mothers were given patosium.

Conception Circumstances

Some babies are conceived in lust rather than love, and this allows demons of lust to enter at the moment of conception. Then there are those who are conceived through rape - even marital rape. A lady brought a young daughter to us for deliverance. The girl was tormented by strong fears, and it was revealed to us by the Holy Spirit that these demons came into her at the point of conception. The mother then told us the circumstances. Her husband had come home drunk,

---

[21]See: *Ministering to Abortion's Aftermath*, Bill and Sue Banks, Impact Christian Books, Inc., 1982.

forcing her to have intercourse. He had held a loaded pistol to her head, coercing her to comply.

Birthing Traumas

Demons take advantage of stress situations in a person's life. When the shield of faith is down, the fiery darts of the evil one are not quenched. Birthing time can be fraught with trauma for both mother and child. Satan knows that he may gain an advantage; therefore, everyone involved needs to "fight the good fight of faith".

We met Steve at a house meeting in North Carolina one summer. He was twenty years of age and had finally graduated from high school. His mother explained that her son had experienced minor brain damage at birth and that he was a slow learner. It had taken Steve two extra years to finish public school. He said that he did not plan to go to college because learning was so difficult for him.

Steve's mother further explained that the umbilical cord was wrapped around his neck at birth, and the oxygen supply to his brain was interrupted for several minutes. Also, she was a heavy smoker while carrying him in her womb.

During our ministry time with Steve, we dealt with spirits of birthing trauma, oxygen deficiency and death. When the spirit of oxygen deficiency was named, the demon cut off Steve's breath, and he began to gasp for air and go limp as though he were dying. The battle was intense but brief. The demons of birthing trauma and nicotine were quickly expelled.

A few months afterward, we received a jubilant letter from Steve's mother. She reported that Steve had not only been delivered, but he was also healed. The function of his brain had been restored greatly. He was no longer hindered in learning and had made application to enroll in college in the fall.

There was severe trauma with the birth of our own daughter, Joyce. Ida Mae developed uremic poisoning, and in her eighth month of pregnancy she was stricken with eclampsia, a serious toxic condition producing convulsions. She was rushed to the hospital, and the baby was delivered by Caesarean section, four or five weeks premature.

Frank was advised by their doctor that the odds were against either Ida Mae or the baby surviving. The small-town hospital had no incubator, and our little four pound daughter grew weaker and weaker. It was decided that we should take the baby to another hospital in a nearby city.

There were further medical complications, and mother and child were separated for a month. Praise God, both survived, but the devil got in his licks.

Sixteen years later, we began to learn about deliverance. Ida Mae was the first person in our church fellowship to receive deliverance, and many of the demons that were cast out of her had gained their entrance through the birthing traumas. Soon afterward our daughter, Joyce, received her deliverance from trauma spirits, and from rejection and insecurity spirits which had taken advantage of the weeks of separation from her mother. She was a serious thumb-sucker until age eight: an outward indication of insecurity.

When people come to us for deliverance, we routinely inquire about any problems associated with their births. Was the cord wrapped? Was it a premature birth? Was it a Caesarean? Were forceps required? Was the labor prolonged? Was there any danger of death? Was there a natural bonding between baby and parents? Did the doctors administer any labor-inducing drugs? (These drugs sometimes affect the baby's nervous system.)

Childhood Wounds And Traumas

The minds and emotions of little ones are extremely vulnerable to wounds and hurts.

Rejection

Rejection, to any degree from conception onward, is one of the most damaging wounds that a child can receive.[22] Of course, intensity and the prolongation of rejection serve to compound the damage. The counselor should reckon that everyone has experienced some degree of rejection at one time or another.

Out of the wounds of rejection there spring many abnormal personality traits, feelings and behaviors. For example, the rejected child will soon begin to manifest traits of insecurity - crying, clinging, thumb-sucking and/or attachment to a crib blanket or a Teddy Bear. As he grows older, one can anticipate that he will react to the wound of rejection with self-pity, hopelessness, rebellion, bitterness, various fears and defensiveness along with distrust and disrespect of authority.

In the formative hours and days of an infant's life, love, and the security it fosters, is provided through tender, touching care. This means that a strong bonding between child and parents is of utmost importance. Furthermore, this bonding must be sustained and maintained. When the bonding tie is disturbed or destroyed, the repercussions can be severe. For example, it is evident to us from our experiences in deliverance (and also recognized by students of psychology) that criminal psychopaths are predominantly the products of rejection, neglect, abandonment and abuse.

---

[22]See: *Overcoming Rejection* by Frank & Ida Mae Hammond

Abuses

Abuse comes in several forms - physical, verbal and sexual. The repercussions of abuse eventually manifest themselves in mental, emotional and behavioral abnormalities.

Whenever the deliverance minister drives out the demons that enter through rejection, abandonment and abuse, he can be confident that he is destroying the roots of many problems, both current and potential, in a child's life.

Fears

Fear spirits are tormentors. Demons of fear may enter through frightening experiences. I (Frank) recall a fear of dogs. When I was five years old, I was playing with a little neighbor girl my same age. While I was pushing her in a coaster wagon, her family's bird-dog came up behind me and bit me on the calf of the leg. It was not a serious wound in my flesh, but a fear of dogs hounded me until I finally received deliverance in my forties!

Night troublers are common: fear of the dark, fear of being left alone, or fear "something is going to get you". We have found such fears rooted in frightening television programs, terrifying experiences, abusive treatment, and in toys and objects in the child's bedroom. One of our foster grandsons, when he was age three, was set free from night terrors after little decals, depicting Casper the Friendly Ghost, were removed from the headboard of his crib.

Dolls and stuffed animals have been found to open a child for familiar spirits: demons that sometimes appear and talk with boys and girls. We recall deliverances where these frightful spirits had gained entrance through likenesses of E.T., Cabbage Patch Dolls, Troll Dolls, various stuffed animals, a mobile of owl figures that glow in the dark and story books about witches and magic.

Family Turmoil

"The dysfunctional family" is a buzz word in our present time. This is psychology's designation for bad performance within the family. From the perspective of biblical truth, a dysfunctional family is one whose members do not produce the fruit of the Holy Spirit -- love, joy, peace, patience, kindness, goodness, faithfulness, gentleness and self-control. Instead, there are "the acts of the sinful nature...sexual immorality, impurity and debauchery; idolatry and witchcraft; hatred, discord, jealously, fits of rage, selfish ambition, dissension, factions and envy; drunkenness, orgies, and the like" Gal. 5:19-23.

Children become prey to marauding spirits when parents are not walking in the light of God's Word. The more flagrant violations include quarreling, fighting, physical abuse, abusive language, neglect, deprivation, abandonment, separation, divorce, adultery, molestation, incest, rape and drugs.

Even in the most exemplary Christian home there can be periods of discord and hurt which undermine the security of the children and breed negative emotions, some of which may be suppressed. In reality, every home is to some degree dysfunctional, for none is perfect.

Divorce

Children's problems within their own personalities and in social relationships have become increasingly aggravated and accented in recent years. When translated into a spiritual context, this means that children are becoming more and more demonized. The disturbance and destruction of the family by divorce is a primary reason for children's trials.

God expects something special from the marriage union: He expects "godly offspring" Mal. 2:15. This is why God hates unfaithfulness in the marriage and why He hates divorce. These transgressions strike at God's hope for a "godly offspring". A complete God-fearing family is the best environment for producing this "godly offspring". God hates divorce, and the unfaithfulness that often precedes it, because of the effect that these circumstances have upon the offspring, robbing God of His rightful inheritance.

> He [God] no longer pays attention to your offerings or accepts them with pleasure from your hands. You ask, "Why?" It is because the Lord is acting as the witness between you and the wife of your youth, because you have broken faith with her, though she is your partner, the wife of your marriage covenant. Has not the Lord made them one? In flesh and spirit they are his. And why one? **Because he was seeking godly offspring**. So guard yourself in your spirit, and do not break faith with the wife of your youth. "I hate divorce," says the Lord God of Israel"... So guard yourself in your spirit, and do not break faith.
>
> Mal. 2:13-16 (Emphasis ours)

God is angry over the innocent victims of divorce whose tears flood the altar of the Lord. He says to unfaithful husbands:

> And this you do with double guilt; you cover the altar of the Lord with tears [shed by your unoffending wives, divorced by you that you might take heathen wives]."
>
> Mal. 2:13, Amplified Bible

The Christian counseling and deliverance ministry has to deal with more and more single-parent situations. After the deliverance is finished, we are compelled to pray that by the grace and mercy of God the children involved be preserved as instruments of righteousness in His Kingdom, and that the single parents be given wisdom and strength to fill the responsibility that God assigned to two parents.

83

Sickness

In a stable family, the members are related to one another is the same way that members of the Body of Christ, His Church, are instructed to relate.

> There should be no division in the body, but that its parts should have equal concern for each other. If one part suffers, every part suffers with it.   I Cor. 12:25,26

When one in the family is sick, the others are concerned and, thereby, are put under pressure. Unless such pressures are faced with trust in Christ and with love toward the hurting member, the devil will have his day.

An infirmity may inflict the child himself or some other member of the household. Sometimes the stress in the home comes through caring for an aged or ailing parent, grandparent or some other relative who needs the love and care of the family.

The special and extra care that one member receives may create jealousy or resentment in the heart of another. Too, the burden of responsibility in caring for an invalid or semi-invalid may touch off emotional upheavals of everything from self-pity and frustration to bitterness and rage. All such impacts upon home life have their repercussions in the lives of children.

Surgeries and Injuries

In reviewing possible trauma times in a child's life, we are looking for the doors through which demons are enabled to enter. How much advantage is given to the devil depends upon the spiritual and emotional maturity with which each incident is met.

Ida Mae has looked death in the face four or five times from various physical crises that have arisen in her lifetime. Her very first deliverance taught us that demons had taken advantage of the pain, the medications, the anesthesia, blood transfusions and other medical procedures.

Consequentially, we were alert to keep a strong spiritual covering over her in subsequent times of physical trauma. Frank would cleanse the hospital room of any and all evil spirits that might have taken up residence there because of what previous patients had experienced in that same room. He prayed and did spiritual warfare over every medical procedure that was administered to Ida Mae. Negative and evil reports were considered spoken curses, and the power of all such words was canceled through the authority of Jesus' name. Demons were driven off at each point of set-back and every new complication. He also ministered something fresh from God's Word each time he visited her in the intensive care unit. He and others anointed her and prayed for her continually. The warfare was like driving away vultures circling over a sick or wounded animal, waiting for their opportunity to alight.

We recommend the same kind of vigilance whenever a child is sick or injured. Times of pain and physical trauma attract evil spirits to the scene. Trips to the doctor or the hospital are trauma times for most children, and the devil knows that such times of anguish may give him an advantage.

> Your enemy the devil prowls around like a roaring lion looking for someone to devour. Resist him, standing firm in the faith.
>
> I Peter 5:8,9

Deaths

Thank God, Jesus has overcome death and the grave. "Death is swallowed up in victory" I Cor. 15:54. This truth is great consolation to those of us who are mature in our faith, but it provides no immediate relief for a young boy or girl whose mother or father or close family member has died. The combination of repercussions is endless: sorrow, grief, heartache, fears, insecurity, loneliness, feelings of abandonment, self-pity, confusion - and on and on goes the list of emotions encountered.

The death of a grandparent, sibling or anyone else who is close can be as painful. We continue to encounter adults who are still suffering from the loss of loved ones during childhood. Demons have tormented them for years. The sorrows of death have become prison bars. We are not able to change the past, but it is not necessary to do so in order to find peace. The Prince of Peace has come:

> To bind up the brokenhearted, to proclaim
> liberty to the captives, and the opening of the
> prison to them that are bound.   Isa. 61:1 KJ

So often, when a family member dies, young children's need for comfort, security and understanding is overlooked. They are little people, and they have feelings, too.

Death not only touches people but pets as well. Children can be very attached to their pets, sometimes overly attached, but that is beside the point here. The death of a dog or cat can be just as traumatic as the death of a close relative. Parents and grown-ups who bear influence in the lives of children should be very alert to help in seasons of death-trauma.

Familiar Spirits

The "familiar spirit" derives his name from his chief characteristic: familiarity. Biblically, familiar spirits are associated with necromancy, divination, witchcraft and spiritist mediums. However, familiar spirits are by no means limited to persons and practices so obviously occult. It is not unusual to find a child who has a familiar spirit otherwise known as an imaginary playmate. This fantasy friend is literally a demon, a familiar spirit. What begins in the child's imagination as a technique to offset loneliness, evolves into a relationship with a familiar spirit.[23]

---

[23]See: *Confronting Familiar Spirits* by Frank Hammond,

Since a demon is a personality, he has the ability to communicate and have a relationship with a human personality. Thus, a child who has an imaginary playmate, with whom he has communication and companionship, has actually developed a relationship with a spirit. This invisible companion is very real to the child. In fact, the playmate may be invisible to others but appear visibly at times to the child. The spirit becomes a companion and a power of influence in the child's life. What begins in the child's imagination as a technique to offset loneliness, can evolve into a relationship with an evil spirit.

Tommy was a four-year-old boy whose father brought him to us for deliverance. The father was having problems with rebellion and disobedience in his son. He explained that whenever he told Tommy to do a certain thing that he would reply, "Charcoal said, 'No', I don't have to do that'". We quickly determined that Tommy had an imaginary playmate named "Charcoal" that was usurping the father's authority and leading this little boy down the path of rebellion and self-will. We asked Tommy why he called his playmate "Charcoal". He insisted that the imaginary playmate told him that his name was Charcoal.

A basic condition to being set free from any spirit is to fall out of agreement with it; therefore, we asked Tommy to tell Charcoal that he had to leave. Tommy was so threatened over the prospect of losing his companion that he stubbornly resisted his father's repeated appeals to renounce Charcoal. Eventually, Tommy complied, and there was a successful deliverance. The next day the father reported that he could already see a marked improvement in Tommy's behavior.

In another case, we ministered to a young woman, Amy, who was beset by troubling supernatural phenomena. Poltergeist manifested themselves in her

The Children's Bread Ministry, 1988.

house. She also experienced unexpected astral travel and possessed disturbing psychic insights. The root cause for all this supernatural activity, in her particular case, was a childhood relationship with an imaginary playmate. Amy had resorted to fantasy escapism at age fourteen after her parents divorced, and she was being passed from relative to relative to be raised. Rejection and insecurity resulted, and Amy sought the companionship of Genie, · an imaginary friend.

Interestingly, Genie (a derivation of jinn) is one of a class of spirits which assumes various forms, exercises supernatural power, and serves his summoner. The familiar spirit, Genie, was responsible for the occult phenomena.

On our second trip into Poland we were glad to see Ewa, a young lady to whom we had ministered personal deliverance on our previous trip to that country. Ewa reported that the victory of her deliverance was short-lived and that she had lost her joy and peace. She was not aware of anything that she had done to cause this loss of victory.

Ida Mae received a word of knowledge that as a child Ewa had an imaginary playmate. Through an interpreter we asked if this was true. She said, "Yes, yes! And her name is Gladys". We explained to Ewa that "Gladys" was a familiar spirit which had kept the door open for the other spirits to return. We then instructed her to dismiss and send Gladys away by telling the familiar spirit that he was no longer wanted or needed as a friend and comforter. We reminded Ewa that the Holy Spirit is her Comforter.

Several days later, as we were preparing to leave Poland, Ewa told us that she was pleased with her ministry and she was rejoicing over her new-found freedom.

We have known of several instances where young children became so caught up in the reality of familiar spirits through their imaginary playmates that they reserved them seats at tables and places next to them when standing in line with others children.

Children's imaginary playmates do not represent cute little games or pastimes; they are dangerous relationships with deceiving spirits.

Demon Groupings

The following list of demon spirits represents those which we frequently encounter: those that are common to children. We have found this catalogue of spirits to be helpful in conducting both individual and group deliverance for children. In every case, THE MINISTRY MUST BE PERSONALIZED. To this end, it is most beneficial, in group deliverance sessions, to have trained workers to personalize individual ministries. **It is a mistake to depend solely on a list of demons.**

I. Inherited Curses:
   1. Causes:
      Idolatry
      Occult practices
      Dishonor of parents
      Disrespect of parents
      Fornication
      Adultery
      Incest
      Bestiality
      Homosexuality
      Lesbianism
      Divorce
      Criminal activities
      Murder
      Abortion
      Suicide
   2. Effects
      Sickness (be specific)
      Poverty
      Insanity

Traumas
Adversities
Failure
Addictions
Barrenness
Struggle

II. Prenatal Influences
Rejection
From mother's influence:
  Fears
  Addictions
  Negative emotions (fear, anxiety, insecurity, depression)
From home environment:
  Conflict
  Quarreling
  Fighting
  Loud, worldly music

III. Birthing Traumas
Cord wrapped
Premature birth
Caesarean birth
Forceps
Prolonged labor
Death threat
Struggle
No bonding
Drug effects:
  Nervous
  Hyperactive
  Tranquilized

IV. Childhood Traumas
Rejection
Abandonment
Abuse
Fears
Family turmoil and pressures
Sickness

Weak
Sickly
Puny
Allergies
Asthma
Infections
Skin diseases
Seizures
Surgeries
Accidents
Deaths (family & friends)
Circumcision (boys):
Occult curses
Ungodly soul ties
Mutilation
School:
Fear of teacher
Fear of tests
Fear of failure
Fear of punishment
Learning difficulties
Embarrassment
Insecurity
Competition
Peer pressure
Persecution
V. Personality and Character Traits
(Developed through reactions to life
experiences and the influence of others --
contrary to the ways of God)
Rejection:
Attention-getting
Fear of rejection
Self-rejection
Refusal to love
Fear of love
Heart-break
Wounded spirit

Loneliness

Misfit

Rebellion:

Self-will

Selfish

Stubborn

Unteachable

Untrainable

Control:

Moods

Temper

Defiance

Holding the breath

Banging the head

Root of bitterness:

Resentment

Hatred

Anger

Memory recall

Retaliation

Violence

Murder

Insecurity:

Timid

Shy

Embarrassment

Self-conscious

Fears of: people, failure, hurt

Lust:

Material: "I want"

Sexual: masturbation, curiosity, nudity,
    obsession, addiction

Guilt:

Self-condemnation

Fear of judgment

Fear of punishment

Fear of exposure

Escapism: Through

Fantasy
Daydreaming
Sleep
Mental illness
Indifference
A closed spirit
Deceit:
Lying
Stealing
Cover-up
Exaggeration
Evasiveness
Self-pity:
Unfairness
Pouting
Criminal:
Fascination with fire (arson)
Stealing
Shop lifting
Kleptomania
Sadistic
Cruel
Destructive
Fascination with weapons (guns, knives, etc.)
Incorrigible
Unruly
Unmanageable
Obstinate
Unyielding
Hopeless
Familiar Spirits:
Imaginary playmates
Occult. From:
Family involvement
Television
Games:
Video

Other
Toys
Dolls
Music
Habits:
Fingernail biting
Thumb sucking
Bed wetting
Hair twisting
Fears of:
The dark
Dogs (other animals)
Insects
Injury
Rejection
Punishment
Being left alone
Doctors
Infirmities:
Weak
Sickly
Puny
Allergies
Asthma
Infections
Skin diseases
Communicable diseases
Procrastination:
Forgetful
Indifferent
Compromise
Lazy

7
SPECIAL CASES

Criminal Schizophrenia

We were ministering in one of the eastern states and were staying in the home of single mother of two young boys.

The mother shared with us the strange problems that she was having with Johnny, her six-year-old. He was a handsome little fellow. Aside from being somewhat hyperactive, it was difficult to imagine the type and degree of problems this mother was describing.

She began by telling us how destructive he was. She said that he destroyed every toy that had ever been given him, within minutes of getting them. If he could not tear them apart with his hands he would hurl them against the wall or floor. He had no appreciation for the value of any material possession.

Another problem was his fascination with fire. He had started several fires that easily could have burned down the house. She now kept all matches safely out of his sight and reach.

But, she had more to report. She had thought perhaps it might help for him to have a pet, so she bought him a cute, little puppy. Johnny was extremely abusive in his treatment of the puppy. He would pull his tail, kick him and choke him. She said that if she had not intervened he would absolutely have killed the dog. She finally gave the dog away before something tragic happened to it. It was not just the dog; he was cruel toward every living creature that he encountered. He seemed to have a sadistic drive to maim or kill everything with which he came in contact.

What really frightened this mother was her son's fascination with weapons. He would not keep his hands off the kitchen knives, so she was vigilant to keep them out of his reach.

The mother asked us to judge something her son had recently acquired from another boy. She had never seen anything like it before. It was a flat metal star about four inches in diameter. The metal points were quite sharp. The boy who gave it to her son said it was a Chinese Star. We had never seen one before, but having just learned about the boy's problems, we knew it wasn't safe for him to have it. Afterward, we inquired around and learned that the Chinese Star is considered a weapon designed to be thrown to injure another person.

This mother was desperate. She had done everything she knew how to do and nothing changed. She had done her best to apply consistent, stringent discipline, but little Johnny did not respond to any kind of punishment. He was unmanageable and non-trainable. He was simply incorrigible.

As we prayed deliverance for Johnny the word "Criminal Schizophrenia" came to Ida Mae as a word of knowledge. Years before, the Holy Spirit had given Ida Mae a revelation on schizophrenia, a network of demons that create the problem that the world calls "schizophrenia", a compound Greek word meaning "divided-mind". Since everyone relates to this particular pattern of spirits to some degree, it is obvious that schizophrenia is a master strategy of the devil. The Bible term for schizophrenia is "double-minded" (James 1:8), from the Greek word *dipsuchos* which means two-souled: a person with two (or more) different personalities.[24]

Over the years we have ministered to people with all sorts of demonic personalities: seductive, vile, devious, cruel, acrimonious, milquetoast, and others. This was a new one to us: criminal! But it made sense.

---

[24]See: *Pigs In The Parlor*, Frank & Ida Mae Hammond, Chapter 21, "The Schizophrenia Revelation".

We are convinced that all schizophrenic personalities are rooted in wounds of rejection, abuse, abandonment and/or betrayal. Rejection leads to self-rejection, and a rejection of "self" results in one becoming a different personality than the one whom God created. The new personality (or personalities) that he takes on is demonic.

Getting back to Johnny, we were told that his father and mother had divorced when Johnny was four, and it was after the divorce that he had become very angry, belligerent and destructive with sadistic tendencies. The break-up of the family caused Johnny to experience the wound of rejection, and this is when all of his problems started. He was now displaying anger and belligerence toward everyone and everything.

About a year later, we received a testimony letter from Johnny's mother telling us that her little boy really had victory over the criminal schizophrenia demons. That one session of deliverance had turned everything around.

After the experience with Johnny, we were made aware of other children who had the same criminal pattern of spirits. Some have been as young as three years of age. Always the root problem has been some traumatic wound in the personality: parents divorcing; rejection, abuse, abandonment and the like.

It is very important that children become bonded to the mother and father at birth. In fact, this bonding should begin before birth through speaking words of loving acceptance to the child in the womb. Once the child is born, touching love and tender care fosters this bonding process. When bonding is denied, frustrated or interrupted, rejection and resulting insecurity is experienced. There are many different repercussions that result from rejection; criminal schizophrenia is only one such possible repercussion.

We are not psychologists, so we do not always use terminology that coincides with psychology. Our terminology comes through the gifts of the Holy Spirit called "the word of knowledge" and "discerning of spirits" I Cor. 12:8,10 KJ. Mental health professionals probably have another designation for what we call "criminal schizophrenia". They may call it psychopathic or sociopathic personality disorder, or something else.

Other facets of criminal schizophrenia found in some individuals are their propensities toward sexual perversions, kleptomania and drug addiction. It is important that this pattern of spirits be dealt with as early in life as possible.

We thank God for the deliverances that we have been able to initiate. The deliverance of children from spirits of criminal schizophrenia breaks up Satan's plot and plan aimed at making them disintegrated personalties, tormentors to their families and menaces to society.

Multiple Personality Disorder

Multiple Personality Disorder, or MPD, is another psychology term that has a bearing on what we label "Criminal Schizophrenia". From our perspective, there is no point in adopting psychology's terminology or adapting to its diagnoses. Psychologists approach human problems from a physiological and psychological perspective, whereas, we approach them as spiritual. They look for chemical imbalances and psychological causes for mental illness and prescribe treatments with drugs and psychotherapy. We, on the other hand, search out spiritual transgressions and wounds and cast out related demons. A problem that is spiritual in origin cannot be resolved by physical and psychological solutions.

Attention Deficit Hyperactive Disorder

Attention Deficit Hyperactive Disorder (ADHD) is yet another term associated with psychology that has gained attention. The characteristics of ADHD are distractibility, impulsiveness and the inability to sit still. Attention Deficit (Hyperactive) Disorder is a new label for an old problem, and more and more parents are asking us, "Is ADHD caused by demons?"

It is unwise to be dogmatic on this issue. Some learning disabilities are due to prenatal brain damage caused by such things as the mother's addictions to alcohol or other drugs. Birthing complications, injuries, high fever and severe sickness are also known to afflict the brain's functions. Further, some mental impairments are genetically inherited. These alternatives mean that deliverance is not always the solution. Some learning problems require a miracle healing.

There are other learning difficulties that are purely physical in origin but which are also compounded by demons. The remedy in such cases is a combination of healing and deliverance. Yet, again, other learning problems are completely demonic, and deliverance is the solution.

When attempting to diagnose learning disorders, it is appropriate to ask, "Is the child receiving needed supervision? Is there orderliness in the home? Do parents provide consistent discipline? Is the child given adequate personal attention"?

What is diagnosed as "attention deficit hyperactive disorder" can be nothing more than an oppression caused by spirits of distraction, hindrances to learning, confusion, mental distress, mind-binding, boredom, day-dreaming, escape from reality or responsibility and troubling memories.

We have observed remarkable results through deliverance in cases of hindrances to learning. We have witnessed the sudden upturn in school grades as proof of children's improved learning ability. Children who have been placed in special education classes have become capable of regular classroom work.

A common error that we often encounter in deliverance circles is the tendency, in unresolved cases, to look for one illusive spirit. It is believed that if this certain spirit can ever be discerned and cast out, then victory will finally come. Some people have criss-crossed the country seeking help from several deliverance ministers in an effort to find the "key" spirit.

More often than not the "key" is getting rid of a pack of "little foxes". There is nothing more effective than an across- the-board approach to deliverance. It is also essential that the demonic roots of a problem be discerned and cast out. Merely lopping off the leaves and limbs, the noticeable parts of a demonic problem, does not bring desired results.

Adopted and Fostered Children

Children who are eligible for adoption or fostering are children who have been cut off from their natural parents. No matter what the circumstances are that create the need for acquiring alternate parenting, and no matter how much love is provided through the adopting and fostering parents, the wound of rejection has occurred and must be cleansed..

Rejection opens up a child for the invasion of evil spirits. The degree of demonization varies widely depending upon other background factors. For example, there are some children who are caught up in the "system", as it is called, of foster home care. They are not placed permanently in one foster home but are shunted from one home to another. This has the same shock effect upon a child that a delicate plant would experience if you uprooted it every day and replanted it in a different soil.

Whenever a child is thrust from one place to another, his emotions take a beating. He must close his emotions to the "family" and atmosphere where he had been "planted" and open them to an altogether new environment with different people and different

100

surroundings. With some children, the stress of repeatedly closing and opening his emotions causes him to permanently close his spirit. He may become an angry, violent, rebellious, non-conforming or withdrawn personality.

This opening and closing of the emotions happens in other childhood circumstances in addition to foster care situations. For example, there are many children of divorced parents who are shuttled back and forth between mom and dad. Each time he leaves one for the other, he must close his emotions to one and open them to the other. The environment in the two homes may be totally different. There are usually step-fathers, step-mothers, step-brothers, step-sisters, half-brothers and half-sisters with whom the child must relate. The two homes may have different rules, different foods, different schedules, different temperaments and different guidelines for discipline. About the time he becomes acclimated to one situation, it is time to switch to the other. Therefore, he begins to shut down his emotions.

Julia was a pre-schooler when we were asked to minister to her. She was withdrawn and "in a shell" so to speak. She could not relate to her father, wanting nothing to do with him. Her father's work required him to be away from home five days of every week. He was only at home on weekends. When dad left home, Julia would cry and feel abandoned, and when he came back home, she would have to open up her emotions to him again. After several years of closing and opening her emotions she had finally shut them down. When father came home, she would not even look at him or acknowledge his presence in any way.

Billy, Bobby and Barry were brothers. Their father and mother had divorced when the boys were two, three and four years of age. They were living with their mother, and their father had dropped out of their lives. Mother had re-married two more times before the boys reached their teens. Prior to her third marriage, the mother was born again and married a fine, Christian man. The boys refused to accept their new step-father as a father, because to them he was just another man who probably wouldn't be in their lives very long. They had closed their emotions to "fathers" and closed their spirits to God. They entered into lives of alcohol, drugs and immorality. We pray that these young men will yet open their hearts to the Lord and receive the help that He has provided through the Cross.

Deliverance is beneficial, but it cannot help until God and the provisions of the Cross are accepted. Jesus pleads,

> Come to me, all you who are weary and burdened, and I will give your rest. Take my yoke upon you and learn from me, for I am gentle and humble in heart, and you will find rest for your souls. Matt. 11:28, 29

There is a bond that is formed between a mother and child by the very fact she has carried that child in her womb for nine months. Whenever this bond is broken, the result is shock and trauma to the child, for it adversely affects his sense of well-being. Since children are totally dependent upon the care of others, they are unsettled by anything that disturbs or destroys their basis of security.

One should also anticipate inherited curses from the sins of the forefathers. Oftentimes few details are known about things in the family backgrounds of adopted and fostered children, and it is really not necessary to know. Simply make a declaration to the devil to the effect that the child is now under the covering of the blood of Jesus. Use your spiritual authority in Christ to take back every advantage that Satan has seized by way of the sins of the forefathers, and cast out every spirit of inherited curse.

In general, recognize the struggles and abnormal behavioral traits in adopted and fostered children, and launch your battle plan from what you observe.

Autism

Autism is not a common problem but a severe one to those afflicted. We have encountered autism a few times in our years of ministry. Autistic children are impaired in their ability to comprehend and communicate. They live in isolation, and many of them are mute. They may appear to be unaware that other people are in their presence. A common trait is an inability to identify with self. The personal pronouns, "I", "me", "my", and "mine" are not used.

Because we are primarily involved in travel ministry, we pray for people, leave town and seldom receive follow-up reports. Sometimes this puts us at a disadvantage in testifying of the lasting fruits of deliverance.

A couple in deliverance ministry shared with us the results of their ministry to a fourteen-year-old autistic boy. He never used personal pronouns. He was not stable enough to go anywhere on his own. When the initial ministry was finished, there was immediate evidence of a breakthrough, for he began to sing: "Jesus loves *me* this *I* know." Days later, his parents reported that for the first time in his life he was able to catch a bus to school without supervision.

Norma, a three-year-old girl was brought for ministry, and Ida Mae prayed for her. She had never spoken any words. The parents had taken her to all sorts of doctors, and they said there was no physical reason why she could not speak. The child was also very hyperactive; always in constant motion. After an hour's ministry the girl lay peacefully in her mother's arms. They brought her to a church service, and she was as relaxed as a rag doll. Her mother and father were awed by the sudden and dramatic change. A few days afterward, we received a letter from the friend who had brought the girl and her parents to us. They were all thrilled. The little girl had spoken a few words. She was saying, "Mama", "Daddy" and "Sister".

It was later reported to us that Norma had shown no further improvement. New medical tests revealed a genetic disorder. Once again we emphasize that deliverance is not the final answer for all problems. Demons take advantage of the disadvantaged; therefore, deliverance can bring about a positive impact upon behavior. Genetic disorders require miracle healing, but we should never forget that Jesus is both Deliverer and Healer. Our faith rests in Him, for with Him nothing is impossible.

Sexual Abuse

The repercussions in a sexually abused child can be varied. In every situation, however, the exploitation opens a child for evil spirits, the most common of which are:

FEARS: insecurity fears, defenselessness, vulnerability, fears of abuse, fears of men/women, and of the night.

LUST: masturbation, pornography, sexual curiosity; sexual experimentation, perversity, harlotry, incubus and succubus, homosexuality and lesbianism.

DEFILEMENT: loss of innocence; unclean

GUILT: self-blame, shame and love-confusion

SOUL TIES

SELF-HATRED

TRAUMA

MEMORY BLOCKAGE

There are tell-tale indications of molestation which do not require supernatural discernment to identify. These include sudden changes in behavioral patterns or a cringing, painful expression on a person's countenance.

Sometimes it is difficult for a seasoned deliverance minister to know for sure whether he is functioning in the gift of discerning of spirits or simply recognizing the presence and nature of certain spirits from having seen their presence manifested over and over on people's countenances. During group deliverance services we have made it a practice to look into the faces of those receiving ministry, and we usually have a "knowing" as to which ones have been sexually molested. A sexual defilement demon commonly betrays his presence through a shame-faced countenance. The person avoids eye contact, keeps the head down and lets his/her hair hand down to cover the face.

Down's Syndrome

Down's syndrome, sometimes called mongolism, is a physical disorder caused by chromosome abnormalities that develop during germ-cell formation. Down's syndrome, and a host of other physical problems, call for miracle healing rather than deliverance. Demons feed on abnormalities, complicating and aggravating them. This is when deliverance is helpful. The vexing spirits that torment and create behavioral problems can be cast out.

Ricky, a four-year-old afflicted with Down's syndrome, was brought to us for ministry by his foster-mother. The foster-mother explained that Ricky would never allow a sock or a shoe on his left foot. To demonstrate this, the mother attempted to put a sock and shoe on the little boy's left foot, and instantly he reached down and yanked them off. He would have nothing to do with them! Interestingly, he was never bothered by a sock or shoe on his *right* foot.

Ida Mae lovingly ministered to Ricky and commanded the vexing spirits to leave his left foot. In order to test the deliverance, first a sock and then a shoe were put on his left foot, and Ricky did not take them off. A follow-up report from the foster-mother a few years later confirmed that there was no further sock or shoe problem. A remarkable change had taken place in Ricky's behavior as a result of the deliverance.

After ministering deliverance to Down's syndrome children we have witnessed marked improvement in levels of function. One, we recall, was a teenager, who, after deliverance surprised his parents with a new ability to answer the phone and convey the messages to others. This is something he had not been able to do before deliverance.

8

A CHILD'S WORLD

There are many factors that influence and fashion the philosophical mind-sets and personalities of children. When one examines and evaluates the myriad of assorted and sordid powers that vie for our children's hearts and minds, we become aware of the demonic overtones in much of it. Thereby, we know that we are confronted by strategies fashioned in hell, and that we are in a real warfare for the salvation of our children.

A missionary-teacher friend of ours, in one of her personal newsletters, related the following:

> On one of my last substitute jobs, I was in a Christian junior high. How happy I was to be where there were Christian students! However, my joy was to be short-lived; the children were as terrible as their peers in the public schools. It really shook me, and I wondered, "Why are these children no different in their behavior?" Now, I think I have the answer: they are watching the same television programs, playing the same games and reading the same books as the unsaved, thus receiving the same destructive influences.[25]

There are indeed many "destructive influences" in the lives of children today that were unheard of in prior generations. The effects of these influences are manifest in the escalation of such social problems as disrespect for authority, promiscuity, teenage pregnancies, abortions, AIDS, gangs, violence, drugs, crime, sadomasochism, homicide and suicide. The devil has declared open warfare against our children and youth. What must the home, the school and the

---

[25]Sally de Arias, *News Letter,* Feb. 1993

church do to counteract Satan's devices and rescue our children from his clutches?

One of the first laws of the battlefield is "know your enemy." The devil is a deceiver and can be depended upon to camouflage his tactics as cleverly as possible so that parents, church leaders and educators will not recognize his cunning schemes.

When Jesus sent his disciples into the world to witness, He counseled:

> I am sending you out like sheep among wolves. Therefore be as shrewd as snakes and as innocent as doves. Matt. 10:16

What does Jesus mean when He says that we are be like serpents? Serpents show great caution and skill in avoiding danger. They are wise in recognizing danger and aggressive in their aptness to oppose it. Thus, we are to be as wise as serpents in both opposing and thwarting the devil's attempts to seduce our children.

"As innocent as doves" literally means that we are to be pure, uncorrupted and sincere. We are not to take on the devil's character nor take up his tactics in our warfare against him. Our weapons are spiritual and not carnal. We do not wrestle against flesh and blood but against unseen spiritual forces in the heavenlies. We must be wise to embrace all that is good and single-minded in opposing all that is evil.

In shedding light on the devil's all-out assault upon our children, it is not our purpose to alarm but to inform; not to frighten but to enlighten. So, what in the world is the devil up to?

New Age In The Classroom

For the past several years we have been hearing much about the New Age Movement, yet we find too many Christians who think that it has nothing to do with them, their families or their communities. Nothing could be further from the truth. New age influence is rapidly invading every segment of society.

The schools are especially targeted, because New Age proponents know that in order to carry out their agenda, the current generation of children must be programmed.

For one thing, New Age proponents advocate "globalism" which, in the classroom, becomes a program to mold the students into one-world consciousness and prepare them for citizenship in a global age. The terminology describing the goals of "one world" proponents includes "interdependence, cooperation, tolerance, empathy, internationalism, distribution of wealth and selflessness". On the surface, these goals sound noble and beyond fault, but the problem comes when these goals are defined and the methods of implementation are unveiled.

Relativism is stressed: the denial of moral absolutes. What is right or wrong is said to be based upon circumstances, personal feelings and preferred consequences. This philosophy opposes the Ten Commandments by denying that God has decreed what is right or wrong. Thus, schools that adopt globalism into their curriculums begin to challenge the spiritual and moral standards upheld by the Church and Christian families.

Furthermore, patriotism and national sovereignty are targeted as evil. The flag of the United States, and the pledge of allegiance to that flag would be replaced with a pledge of allegiance to the United Nations and its flag. Globalists espouse liberal politics. Also, one-world government is essential to the goals of globalism.

"Some global educators preach a new religion for the world based on Eastern mysticism. In fact, global education is the political side of the New Age coin".[26] Those who believe that the Bible is the inspired Word

---

[26]Bueher, Eric (1990), *The New Age Masquerade* (The Hidden Agenda In Your Child's Classroom), Wolgemuth & Hyatt, Brentwood, Tenn. p. 29.

of God and that Jesus Christ is the only way of salvation are labeled as bigots and fools, for they are a threat to the New Age objective of one religion. One-world religion is as important as one-world government, both of which prepare the way for the coming Antichrist.

Through New Age programs, children are introduced to such occult practices as altered states of consciousness, yoga meditation, guided imagery, visualization, hypnotism, necromancy (communication with the dead), contact with familiar spirits (who are said to be "imaginary guides" or "walk-in spirits" from whom they are instructed to seek wisdom and decision-making guidance) and the development of psychic powers.

Public schools in Los Angeles, California, already have conducted pilot programs introducing global philosophy through occult practices.[27] If such programs are allowed to spread, multiplied thousands of children will be opened to demon possession.

Christians must stay informed and keep abreast of what is being taught in the public schools. Occult activities in the classroom may come through the curriculum or through teachers who are practicing occultists. In some situations, parents and church leaders must take the initiative to educate local educators on the hidden motives and goals of global education.

---

[27]Ibid, pp 83-108.

9

THE BATTLE FOR THE

IMAGINATION

Toys and games that draw upon a child's imagination are a big part of his life and rightly so, for this is how he learns to relate to the world around him. A little girl plays with her dolls and pretends that the doll is her baby, thus instilling in herself the qualities of motherhood. A little boy plays with his toy cars and trucks and sees himself as a grown-up. Perhaps he will be a fireman or a truck driver. A child's mind is like a sponge, soaking up anything and everything it encounters. The images he absorbs become building blocks of future life decisions for his place in the world.

Imagination is a gift from God. It can be influenced for good or perverted for evil depending upon outside influences. The major influences in a child's life are: parents, peers, toys, television, movies, books, video games, magazines and music.

Parental care is the primary influence in a child's life, provided the parent spends quality time with his child. If little Johnny or Susie is placed in a Day Care Center and in the evening is picked up, fed and put to bed or deposited in front of a television, the parent will have very little positive influence on him. The world system will have become his teacher and example.

Children spend much of their time in a world of make- believe. They can be whatever their fertile imaginations create. A child should give animation to his toys out of real life experiences, rather than from imitation of a cartoon character.

Children frequently project themselves into their toys. If their toys are of an occult nature, and they continually pretend to be mystical characters performing magical feats, they are likely to be drawn in to the reality of their fantasies. Herein lies a horrible danger. Occult fantasies guide a child into the realm of Satan.

Therefore, it is important that parents and teachers provide children with games and toys that guide their imaginations in wholesome, creative and godly ways. It is wise to avoid books, games, television programs and toys which present occult, sexual or violent images. Otherwise, there will be a subtle deception by which layer upon layer of satanic influence will program their minds, drawing them more and more into Satan's kingdom.

Unless Christian values are instilled in the hearts and minds of our children, by the time they reach their teens they will have more knowledge of the occult, Eastern mysticism, violence and perverted sex than they will of God. Already, we see a generation growing up with attitudes and behaviors that oppose God and His Word.

The more unstable a child's home life, the more rejection and insecurity he perceives. Thereby, he becomes more drawn to the evil influences that surround him. In order to compensate for rejection, abuse and neglect he will pursue fantasies that feed his ego. He will imagine himself to have mystical powers, sexual prowess and physical invincibility. He will more than likely seek the fulfillment of fantasies through involvement in such activities as the occult, pornography and the martial arts.

Unmasking Toys, Games & Television Programs

Have you walked through a toy store lately? If so, you probably found yourself surrounded by evil and demonic looking characters, and you probably felt that you had been thrown suddenly into the abyss with Satan and all of his demons. It is shocking to see what is being offered to our children for playthings. Notice how many of today's toys are blatantly associated with wickedness of every sort: witchcraft, violence, murder, barbarianism, the grotesque, the bizarre and the occult.

Who is behind the creation of such evil? Many of today's toys are designed and manufactured by people of the 60's generation. This was a decade of young men and women who smoked marijuana, took mind trips on L.S.D. and who sat for hours in the lotus position practicing transcendental meditation and communing with demons.

In all probability they saw the very demons whose likeness they now present to our children. We have ministered to people of the "Hippie" generation who related nightmarish encounters with hideous demonic beings.

The following is a list of toys which portray occult and witchcraft practices and encourage a child's participation in them. These top selling toys are spin-offs of movies and video games of the same name. Keep in mind that, as a child plays with them, he fantasizes himself as being able to do all and perhaps more than the actual characters do.

DUNGEONS & DRAGONS: A fantasy game fought in the mind of the player. D&D teaches demonology, witchcraft, voodoo, murder, rape, blasphemy, suicide, assassination, insanity, sexual perversion, Satan worship, barbarianism, cannibalism, sadism, demon summoning, necromancy, divination and human sacrifice. Role playing can result in a person taking on a demonic personality of the character played.

RAINBOW BRITE AND SPRITES: Although Rainbow Brite is presented as a cute little girl, she has magical means of travel. Rainbow Brite casts spells and uses mind control. The cartoon series is filled with occult symbolism. Sprites, the cheerful little creatures who mine and manufacture *Star Sprinkles,* are disembodied spirits.

PEGASUS: A mythical flying horse from the Dungeon & Dragons monster manual. Pegasus originated in Greek mythology, and is said to have been born of the blood of the decapitated Medusa.

UNICORNS: These mythical creatures are also monsters listed in the Dungeon & Dragons manual. Medieval kings and popes used amulets supposedly made from its horns. They believed it had magical and healing powers. The unicorn is a long-standing occult beast of a schizophrenic nature - at one time docile and loving, laying its head in the lap of a maiden; then aggressive and violent in goring its enemies to death.

CARE BEARS: There is a bear for each emotion of a child. Care Bears usurp the relationship between parent and child by transferring the love and security of the parent to an inanimate object. Magic and tenets of Eastern religion are interwoven in the stories. Dark Heart casts spells.

CABBAGE PATCH DOLLS: These dolls create a demonic soul tie with the child by means of an oath which is issued with each doll. The humanizing of these dolls is taken to the point where a child views the doll as real. When the line between make-believe and reality is blurred or obliterated, the child is opened to accept a familiar spirit. Also, the humanizing of these dolls makes mockery of life, death, adoption, weddings, funerals and even water baptism. This is blasphemy and idolatry.

BARBIE DOLLS: On the 25th Anniversary of Barbie, her designer was quoted in news releases as saying he was sorry that he had ever made her. He felt the doll was responsible for many young women becoming anorexic. We concur. Also, many young women suffer from self-hatred and self-rejection because their bodies are not perfectly shaped like the Barbie they idolize.

GREMLINS: They are violent, grotesque, sadistic and cannibalistic. They also employ transformation which is a New Age concept. Webster defines *gremlin* as: "a creature supposed to interfere with the smoothness of any procedure". Thus, a gremlin represents a curse.

SWORD AND SORCERY BATTLE GEAR: A fantasy of sorcery, the occult and violence.

STARRIORS: Warrior robots kill for control of the earth using chain saws, buzz saws, drills, spikes, reams and a vibrator chisel. Starriors are extremely violent.

SECRET WARS: In this game one fights aliens with "the force", a counterfeit of God. There are wild mutants and hideous creatures.

OTHER WORLD: This game is similar to Dungeons and Dragons. The player battles with warlords, demons and dragons. It is violent.

MASTERS OF THE UNIVERSE: Skeletor is an evil lord of destruction, beastmen and evil goddesses. It is based upon sorcery and witchcraft.

SNAKE MOUNTAIN: The player acts like a snake while working the snake's jaws as it speaks. The child pretends to be a snake.

ROBO FORCE: An evil robot empire. It has a killer instinct and a crusher hand. Robo Force is a dictator and destroyer. It is very violent. Other transformer toys are Voltron, Robotech, GoBots and Transformers. The evil of such toys is not easily discerned until they are observed in their corresponding cartoons, then their extreme violence is seen along with occult overtones and, in some, sexual implications.

NINJA TURTLES: They employ violent force of will, skill and power to conquer their enemies. Their supernatural abilities are derived from occult sources coupled with martial art skills. They rely upon power derived from devotion to spiritual superiors. Their fighting prowess is derived from New Age techniques of telepathy, visualization and conjuring. They have the ability to become invisible.

The movie, Teenage Mutant Ninja Turtles, used Eastern meditation and divination. It referred to "The Force" as a power that bound them together and brought Splinter to them to speak to them out of their campfire. "The Force" is associated with witchcraft, and in Star Wars "The Force" could be manipulated through mind control. This is the philosophy of Zen Buddhism which is contradictory to Christian belief that God is sovereign. Fallen man is dependent upon God Almighty for his salvation; he cannot control or command God as he wills.

SUPER NATURALS: These characters display powers of divination through insight into the future. Other occult powers include snake charming and hypnotism. Witchcraft is brought in through pentagram (witchcraft) power released by each toy. Books that accompany the toys carry occult stories.

SUPERNATURAL SPOOKS: The following description is printed on the toy boxes: "A different kind of supernatural. The tomb of doom is open after hundreds of years, free at last. Heroic and evil warriors with strange and mysterious powers lead armies of spirit ghostlings into our world. Can earth survive the battle of the supernaturals?"

ALIEN BLOOD AND MONSTER FLESH: This is sold in cans!

MAD SCIENTIST MONSTER LAB: The child is encouraged to make disgusting, gross monsters and then sizzle the flesh off their bones.

VISIONARIES: This toy features Knight of the Magical Light. Extar has a mystical personality with magical holographic power to see the enemy. This figure represents witchcraft and divination.

GHOST BUSTERS: Banshee Ghost Bomber drops Ecto-Plazam on its victim. Ecto-Plazam (ectoplasm) "in spiritism is the vaporous luminous substance

116

supposed to emanate from the medium's body during a trance" (Webster's New Universal Unabridged Dictionary). This is blatantly occult.

MY LITTLE PONIES: A half-man half-goat creature wants the ponies to pull his Chariot of Darkness. They go to a wizard for help. This is also blatantly occult. Darkness is the nature of Satan's kingdom.

MOON DREAMERS: Magic dream crystals make wishes come true when given by Dream Gazer, the mystical sorceress. This bears a New Age occult concept.

SMURFS: These little creatures originated in Germany. Their pale blue color represents death. They bear a strong occult influence upon children. Papa Smurf is a wizard. He cast spells and mixes potions to help the other Smurfs. He is the counterpart to Baalzebub (Satan). Another character is Gargamel, a wizard, who chants a spell while dancing on a pentagram (a five-pointed star associated with witchcraft).

Through playing with occult toys and fantasizing occult activities, a child becomes familiar with the satanic supernatural. It is a simple transition from the imagined to the real world of demonic activities.

TROLLS: Trolls are either giants or dwarf-like creatures which originated in Scandinavian folklore. They inhabit hills, caves or live underground. Webster's New Collegiate Dictionary defines *troll* as a "demon".

E.T. (EXTRA TERRESTRIAL): E.T., a hideous looking alien being, was made into a movie in 1982. The movie began with several boys playing *Dungeons and Dragons*, a very dangerous occult game. The movie version of E.T. employs many occult symbols and utilizes levitation and mental telepathy, common practices of spiritism. When E.T. dies, he resurrects himself and ascends back to his own planet, a counterfeit of the resurrection and ascension of Jesus Christ. E.T. is a demon and not God! The story presents the deception that only children can understand E.T. Children are taught to protect E.T. by keeping secret his presence, and not telling their parents. The whole plot conveys the fallacy that superior beings have evolved on other planets in the universe.

We recall ministering to a young boy who told us that E.T. had visited him in his bedroom. The child was not at all frightened, but instead he considered this experience a visit from one of his friends. Such events vividly illustrate the dangerous influence of occult laden toys, games, television programs and movies. Cute, ugly and weird little characters become familiar friends who can later manifest themselves as familiar spirits. We estimate that one third of the children to whom we minister have been "visited" by either one or more of their fantasy friends.

Board Games

Board games are another popular way for children to get drawn into the occult. These games introduce children to the influence of wizardry, violence, mind control and witchcraft. Children often receive the following games as Christmas and birthday presents: Thundar Barbarian, Pandemonium, Magic 8 Ball, Monster Mansion, Krull, Herself the Elf, Gremlins, Dragon Master, Mythical Cards, Dungeon, Dungeon And Dragons, Ouija, Dark Towers, Magical Crystals, Dragon Lords, Towers of Night, Forest of Doom, Fires of Shadarr, Star Wars and Yoda, Fantasy Card Game, Hell Pits of Night Fang, Rune Quest, Chivalry, Sorcery and Arduin-Grimoire. Their very names betray their evil nature.

Video Games

Warning! There has been a marriage of electronics and the occult. It has birthed everything from computerized demonology to seemingly harmless but powerfully seductive video games.

These games are as progressively addictive as drugs. Young players usually start out with the less violent ones such as Donkey-Kong, Pac-Man and Smurf. Tiring of these easy games, the children progress on to more challenging ones which often provide increased emphasis upon violence and occultism.

Video games are becoming more and more sophisticated. They have become so specialized that they draw players right into the contest by providing sensory output, so realistic that the player is caught up in the illusion that he is a part of the action and forgets that he is only playing a game. It is dangerous mental deception when fantasy appears as reality.

NINTENDO
A CRAZE THAT IS HYPNOTIZING A GENERATION
By Shirley Smith

There is a war going on against our children in almost every area of their lives. Entertainment is one major area. I believe video-games are one of the main tools being used by Satan to seduce, hypnotize, desensitize and addict our children. They are confronted with excessive and extreme violence, as well as the occult in these games. As a result, violent action, even murder, has victimized some of our children.

In the March 6, 1989, "NEWSWEEK" magazine, the cover states, "The Nintendo Craze Hypnotizing A Generation." The article states, "The Nintendo is a toy, but it is more than a toy; it is a whole new medium, an immensely powerful agent for the dissemination of culture." They describe it as "an oblong plastic box that sits on top of the television set, about the size of a family Bible." It's interesting that they use this comparison, when families should be spending time in the Bible together. It's appalling that the secular world sees the effect and damage it is doing to our children. I wonder why our Christian parents, pastors, youth leaders, and teachers are not seeing this.

My concern now is about these ever-popular NINTENDO GAMES.

HOME ARCADES: Arcades were once the most popular place to be. But now parents have moved the Arcades into their homes, and children have full, unrestricted access to them. Few parents realize what they have done. The majority of these games their children are playing have progressively seduced, mesmerized and desensitized them to violence, pain and even death. Most of the games hinge on "kill or be killed" themes. But more serious than this is the fact that at least 75% of these games are complete with teachings on the BLACK ARTS of the OCCULT. For example, these games encourage your children to become snared and involved with the following occult things. They are taught to accept them as mere toys and harmless imaginations. Here is a partial list of what your child is playing with:

DEVILS, DRAGONS, BABYLON, MYSTERIOUS FORCES, MYTHICAL BEASTS, MYTHICAL GODS, WIZARDS, WARRIORS, MAGIC POWER, BLACK PRINCES, MINIONS OF HELL, MAGIC SCROLLS, EVIL MONSTERS, MAGIC ITEMS, BAALZEBUB,

ECTOPLASM, CURSE OF DEATH, EVIL
SPIRITS, BLACK MAGIC, MAGICAL
SCROLLS, DRUIDS, WITCHCRAFT, EVIL
WIZARDS, SORCERY, POTIONS, DEMONS,
CURSES, NECROMANCY, HOLY WATER,
BUDDHA, MONSTERS, MAGICAL SPELLS,
MAGICAL SWORDS, MAGICAL BOOKS,
BEASTS, WANDS AND WITCHES.

Are you SHOCKED?? Do you wonder where I got
these descriptive words and information? They were
written on the backs of the boxes that the
NINTENDO GAMES come in. Each game has a
legendary story, MYTH OR FABLE. You may
check these out for yourself at the nearest store that
sells these games.

Satan is very active with his deceptive tactics. It is
obvious that he has targeted our present generation of
children and youth. He is infiltrating the minds,
emotions, bodies and spirits of our young people with
the spiritual poison of materialism, the occult and
Eastern religious philosophy.
We Westerners are at a disadvantage in attempting
to understand the influx of Eastern philosophy,
dress, religion and mysticism into our culture
through the New Age Movement. The
funny-looking creatures that come at our kids
through the cartoons are viewed by most of us as
"just another fad". In this way, we have been
disarmed. By the time we figure things out, the
Eastern hook has already been firmly imbedded into
the soul of our child. Subconsciously, he/she is then
vulnerable and suggestible to the voices that will
speak to him/her, in later years, to reject Christ and
embrace paganism ... I pray that our parents will
become very discriminating about what goes into the
minds of their children. Remember that every
experience of life is taken into the subconscious and
recorded there for all time --- and that includes every

movie and TV show, book and coloring book that they are exposed to.[28]

New toys, games and television shows for children are being produced at an astounding rate. The listing we have presented in this chapter will soon be outdated. Other authors seem called to the task of analyzing and cataloguing new ones as they appear. Our objective is to give examples of the evil influences found in entertainment items for our children, to alert parents to the dangers to and provide guide-lines for evaluating whatever manufacturers offer.

Summary of Negative Influences Upon Children
What is detrimental to a child's spiritual, mental, psychological, emotional and physical well being? All toys, games, television programs, computer games, comics, movies, books, rock music and public school teachings that have anything to do with Eastern mysticism, witches, wizards, witchcraft, mediums, seances, charms, sorcery, hexes, spells, curses, hypnosis, clairvoyance, mental telepathy, telekinesis, trolls, gremlins, astrology, zodiac, horoscopes, channeling, necromancy, divination, enchantments, elves, fairies, extra terrestrials, martial arts, yoga, visualization, guided imagery, values clarification, globalism, multiculturalism, pagan rites, journaling, spirit guides, violence, rebellion, supernatural manipulation or control, as well as other similar things.

What should parents do whose children are already attached to some of the things we have mentioned? First, be convinced in your own heart and mind that these things are evil and have no place in your children's lives. You cannot act in faith on another person's conviction; you must have your own. There are other Christian writers who are voicing the same

---

[28]Dr. William Probasco, *Heart To Heart*, Ninja Turtles; Hooking The Children On The Occult.

warnings. Read their books, or do your own research, if necessary.

Second, pray for God's wisdom and guidance as to how to inform your children that you are now opposing what you have previously approved or tolerated. It is very unwise to destroy, throw out and ban things to which your children are strongly attached without proper preparation through parental repentance and thorough communication. Unless a child has understanding that brings him to the place of cooperation, more harm than good can result. For example, watch questionable television programs with your child, analyzing them and judging them in the light of Truth. Examine together the weird names and terminology associated with their toys, games, books and music.

Third, replace evil things with good things. Be certain that a vacuum is not left in your child's life. He has a right to playthings and entertainment; the parent's responsibility is to see that these are edifying and wholesome.

Fourth, take time daily to instill the principles of God's Word into the mind and conscience of your child. Set the right example before him. Teach him to love the Lord with all his heart, soul, mind and strength. God's advice to the families of Israel through Moses is especially timely today:

> These commandment that I give you today
> are to be upon your hearts. Impress them on
> your children. Talk about them when you sit
> at home and when you walk along the road,
> when you lie down and when you get up.
>
> Deut. 6:6,7

Some children are quick to respond to truth as soon as they hear it; others are not so readily convinced. Patience and persistence bathed in love are the virtues that can make the difference in dealing with the child who is struggling with the decision to obey God.

Parents, let's not lose sight of the fact that the devil has an agenda to capture our children. He is a master of deception. We must take the offensive against him.

The New Age movement is a primary vehicle that the devil is using to program today's younger generation for the advent of one-world government and a one-world religious order. These things will come abouot under the rule of the Antichrist who will deceive many through the very occult powers that are made attractive to our children through worldly influences.

Finally, it is imperative that children be delivered from the demon spirits which have invaded their lives.

10

OCCULT INFILTRATION

What does God's Word say about occult practices? God does not leave us in doubt. The Canaanites were ripe for God's judgment due to their abominable occult practices; therefore, God dispossessed these nations and gave their land to the Israelites. Then God said to His people:

> When you enter the land the Lord your God is giving you, do not learn to imitate *the detestable ways* of the nations there. Let no one be found among you who sacrifices his son or daughter in the fire, who practices divination or sorcery, interprets omens, engages in witchcraft, or casts spells, or who is a medium or spiritist or who consults the dead. *Anyone who does these things is detestable to the Lord,* and because of *these detestable practices* the Lord your God will drive out those nations before you. You must be blameless before the Lord your God. The nations you will dispossess listen to those who practice sorcery or divination. *But as for you, the Lord your God has not permitted you to do so.*
> Deuteronomy 18:9-13 (Emphasis ours)

Parents of young children urgently need to familiarize themselves with common terms, definitions and Scriptures pertaining to occult practices. This will, in turn, help parents to teach their children to identify and discern occult deceptions which come across their paths.

We must be diligent to train our children to discern good and evil and to hear the voice of the Holy Spirit for themselves, so that maturity in age will coincide with spiritual maturity.

The writer of Hebrews reminds us:

> Anyone who lives on milk, being still an infant, is not acquainted with the teaching about righteousness. But solid food is for the mature, **who by constant use have trained themselves to distinguish good from evil.** Heb. 5:13,14, (Emphasis ours).

Parents will not always be there to tell their children right from wrong, so children must be trained to judge and decide for themselves. Legalism, with its rigid rules of do's and don'ts, nurtures rebellion. This is why many children, when they grow up and get on their own away from parental supervision, act out their suppressed rebellion. They throw off the restraints of religious legalism, become worldly and grow cold toward God and the Church. We have seen parents of such children become confused and frustrated. What went wrong? Does not God's Word promise? "Train a child in the way he should go, and when he is old, he will not turn from it" Prov. 22:6.

God's way of training requires the constant exercise of an individual's spiritual senses so that he will train himself to discern good from evil. When a child is rightly trained, he will listen to the voice of the Spirit in times of temptation; and, when he is confronted with the allurements of the occult, his spiritual senses will have been trained "to distinguish good from evil" Heb. 5:14.

Some of the occult terms found in Scripture are quite specific while others are generalizations. From God's viewpoint, which should also be our own, occult practices violate the first commandment: "You shall have no other gods before me" Exod. 20:3. In Deuteronomy 18 such practices are labeled "detestable ways", and God's people are warned "not to learn to imitate" them. v.9. The following is a list of occult terms together with a brief definition of each. Bible references are given for terms (or their equivalents) which occur in Scripture.

1. **Astral projection; astral travel:** The illusion of one's spirit leaving his body and traveling to another place or time. This is a witchcraft event that is orchestrated by demon spirits.

2. **Astrology:** ("Observer of times", Deut. 18:10, 14). A form of augury. The pseudo science which claims to foretell the future of human affairs by studying the relative positions of the sun, moon and stars. Lev. 19:26b; Deut. 18:10, 14 KJ; II Kgs. 21:6 KJ; II Chron. 33:6 KJ.

3. **Augury:** The art of foretelling events by signs or omens.

4. **Charmer (vb. to charm):** A magician; one who has or uses the power of enchantment to control another person by means of word, action, song, gesture or object; a hypnotist; one who puts a spell on another. Deut. 18:11 KJ; Ps. 58:5; Isa. 19:3 KJ.

5. **Diviner; Divination (vb. to divine):** A fortuneteller; a prognosticator. One who tries to predict events or reveal the unknown by occult techniques. Deut. 18:10, 14; II Kgs. 17:17; Jer. 27:9; Jer. 29:8; Acts 16:16-18.

6. **Enchanter (enchantment):** One who uses charms and engages in magical arts; who whispers as a sorcerer (uses either their voice or music to bring another person under psychic control) or makes auguries (foretells events by signs and omens). Exod. 7:11 KJ; Lev. 19:26b KJ; Deut. 18:10-12 KJ; II Chron. 33:6 KJ; Eccl. 10:11 KJ; Isa. 47:9 KJ; Dan. 1:20; Jer. 27:8-9; II Kgs. 17:17 KJ; II Kgs. 21:6 KJ.

7. **Clairaudience:** The power to hear voices or perceive sounds not normally audible. This is experienced through hypnotic trance.

8. **Clairvoyance:** The power to see into another place while in a hypnotic trance; seeing objects that are not

perceptible to the normal senses.

9. **Levitation:** To cause an object or body to rise in the air by meditation and calling upon demonic supernatural power or force for assistance in overcoming gravity.

10. **Magic (magician):** Sorcery. The art of producing desired effects or controlling events by use of various techniques, as incantations, spells and rituals that presumably assure human control of supernatural agencies or forces of nature. Power to influence through charming. Gen. 41:8, 24; Dan. 2:10,27; 4:7,9; 5:11.

11. **Necromancy (necromancer):** [consults the dead]; Conjuration, sorcery and witchery. The Hebrew word means "to seek; to inquire" in reference to those who seek to foretell the future through communication with the dead. A necromancer is a spiritist medium who communicates with familiar spirits which impersonate the dead. Deut. 18:11; I Sam. 28:1-25; I Chron. 10:13-14; Isa. 8:19.

12. **Pass through the fire:** Child sacrifice. The practice by ancient Canaanites of sacrificing their children to Molech, a sun god related to Baal. The idol was a brazen statue with a bull's head which was hollow and capable of being heated, with arms stretched out to receive the children to be sacrificed. Children were laid in the heated arms and burned. The spirit of Molech (child sacrifice) is the spirit which today advocates and practices abortion. Lev. 18:21; Deut. 18:10

13. **Poltergeist:** A German word meaning "noisy ghosts". These are spirits which manifest their presence by knocking, table rapping and other mysterious noisy disturbances.

14. **Prognostication:** To foretell from signs or symptoms. To prophesy without the Holy Spirit. Isa. 47:13 KJ.

15. **Soothsaying:** Includes various acts of computing and divining to foretell the fortunes and destinies of individuals, such as observing the clouds for the purpose of augury. The ancient Chaldeans cast nativities (horoscopes at the time of one's birth) to determine and decree the fate and destiny of a person. Thus, the act of foretelling events and prophesying by a spirit other than the Holy Spirit. Josh. 13:22 KJ; Isa. 2:6 KJ; Dan. 2:27 KJ; 4:7 KJ; 5:56,11 KJ; Mic. 5:12 KJ; Acts 16:16 KJ.

16. **Sorcery (sorcerers):** The practice of magic arts with an intent to do mischief to men or beasts; or to delude and pervert the mind. The Greek word translated "sorcerer" is *magus* from which the word "magician" is derived. "Elymas the sorcerer", Acts 13:8, was a wizard, and a professor of the arts of witchcraft. Exod. 7:11; Isa. 47:9; Jer. 27:9; Dan. 2:2; Mal. 3:5; Acts 8:9; 13:6,8; Rev. 9:21 KJ; 21:8 KJ.

17. **Telekinesis:** The employment of evil spirits to move an object which is not in contact with the body of the person generating the force.

18. **Telepathy:** The employment of evil spirits to communicate between minds apart from normal sensory channels.

19. **Witchcraft:** The power or practices of witches. The use of magic formulas, paraphernalia and incantations to practice sorcery. Exod. 22:18; Deut. 18:10; I Sam. 15:23 KJ; 2 Kgs. 9:22; II Chron. 33:6; Mic. 5:12; Nah. 3:4; Gal. 5:20.

11

BEYOND DELIVERANCE

How does it happen that children have demons in the first place? Since parents are the protectors and providers for their offspring, the presence of evil spirits in a child is, to a large degree, a reflection upon the parents. Demons cannot enter unless doors of opportunity are opened to them. Parents are the gate-keepers: guardians and maintainers. When a child has demons, it indicates that his parents either did something wrong or neglected to fulfill their responsibility.

Our daughter was a teenager when the Lord brought us into the knowledge of deliverance. After the two of us had experienced our own deliverances, we began to think about our daughter's needs. We said, "Joyce, we are responsible for most of the demons that you have in you, so we should have the privilege of casting them out." She agreed, and the Lord permitted us to be the instruments of her deliverance.

The majority of us parents readily admit that we are guilty of mistakes and neglect. However, this is no time for a guilt trip. There is help in God, and the important thing is that we take advantage of the grace of God poured out through the substitutionary death of Jesus Christ. Deliverance is one of the benefits of the cross.

> When evening came, many who were demon-possessed where brought to him, and he drove out the spirits with a word and healed all the sick. This was to fulfill what was spoken through the prophet Isaiah: "He took up our infirmities and carried our diseases".   Matt. 8:16,17

Both of us had good, caring, Christian parents, and they would have gone to any length to make things better for their children. In those days, however, deliverance was unheard of in their churches, but deliverance has been restored to the Body of Christ in this present generation. Today, there is much teaching and plenty of opportunity for families to learn about and experience deliverance.

Whenever we announce deliverance services for children we always get a good response from parents. This action speaks well of the desire of Christian parents in general to remedy past mistakes and do whatever they can to insure future blessings. What needs to be done beyond deliverance?

Let us kept in mind that the casting out of demons is not an instant and complete cure for all problems. As important and vital as it is, deliverance does not absolve parents from their responsibilities toward their children. Other things must accompany and complement deliverance in order to make it effective and to retain all that is gained through it.

Provide a Stable Home Environment

Strife, division, rejection, abuse and neglect create a home environment in which demons thrive. Deliverance is not a substitute for a godly home. Children are the products of the home. They become whatever they are brought up to be.

> Train a child in the way he should go, and
> when he is old he will not turn from it.
> Proverbs 22:6

Children are deeply affected and their personalities molded by the emotional and spiritual environment in the home. In the majority of cases, when the husband is a wife-abuser, his sons will follow the same pattern. When the mother is disrespectful of her husband, the daughters will follow her example into marriage.

The majority of demons found in adults entered them in childhood. When things are not right in the home, the devil has his opening. This is a loud and clear warning that we must major on the strengthening of the family. God's Word gives His plan for family order, and only when the family is set in Divine order and functioning faithfully in that order, will the members of the family be protected from the invasion of marauding spirits.

In simple terms, God's plan, which is an extension of His righteous Kingdom and the delegation of Divine authority, is outlined as follows:

1. The husband/father must bear headship under Christ, functioning as Christ's representative and be prepared to give an account to the One who has placed him in authority. Husbands are specifically charged to: "love your wives, just as Christ loved the church and gave himself up for her" Eph. 5:25. Fathers are commanded: "Do not exasperate your children; instead, bring them up in the training and instruction of the Lord" Eph. 6:4.

2. The wife/mother must respect the God-ordained headship of the man, submitting herself to him for the good of family order and function. As a wife she is specifically instructed: "The wife must respect her husband" Eph. 5:33b; "Be submissive to your husbands so that, if any of them do not believe the word, they may be won over without talk by the behavior of their wives, when they see the purity and reverence of your lives" I Peter 3:1-2.

3. Children are instructed: "Obey your parents in the Lord, for this is right. 'Honor your father and mother' - which is the first commandment with a promise - that it may go well with you and that you may enjoy long life on the earth" Eph. 6:1-3.[29]

---

[29]See: *Kingdom Living For The Family* by Frank & Ida Mae Hammond, Impact Christian Books, Inc. 1985

Provide Proper Discipline

Discipline for children includes corporal punishment, but involves much more. Webster defines "discipline: 1: to punish or penalize for the sake of discipline 2: to train or develop by instruction and exercise esp. in self-control 3: to bring under control; to impose order upon".[30]

Hebrews 12:7-11 helps us to understand discipline from God's perspective:

> Endure hardship [chastening] as discipline; God is treating you as sons. For what son is not disciplined by his father? If you are not disciplined (and everyone undergoes discipline), then you are illegitimate children and not true sons. Moreover, we have all had human fathers who disciplined us and we respected them for it. How much more should we submit to the Father of our spirits and live! Our fathers disciplined us for a little while as they thought best; but God disciplines us for our good, that we may share in his holiness. No discipline seems pleasant at the time, but painful. Later on, however, it produces a harvest of righteousness and peace for those who have been trained by it. Heb. 12:7-11, Brackets are from the King James translation.

Everyone needs discipline as proof of his sonship. God's hand of discipline proves His love and reveals that we are His children. The Heavenly Father is the pattern for earthly fatherhood. A good earthly father will establish discipline: good, wholesome, loving, corrective, instructive, mature discipline in the home.

Deliverance never takes the place of discipline; it only supplements it.

One must "endure chastening as discipline". The willingness and determination to endure chastening must be woven into the character of a child's

---

[30]Webster's' Seventh New Collegiate Dictionary, G&C Miriam Co., Chicago, IL, 1963, p. 237.

personality. There are many times and situations when we must encourage our children: "All right, let's learn to endure. Let's not curl up; let's not give up; let's not stop trying or quit."

In order to have a family that can overcome adversity, endurance must be taught and exemplified by the parents. There are many opportunities to test endurance: dysfunctional parents, family squabbles, sibling rivalry, personality conflicts, violation of privacy and responsibilities that chafe the flesh.

"God is treating you as sons. For what son is not disciplined by his father?" v. 7b. Notice that God speaks to fathers rather than mothers. It is the father's responsibility to set the standard and pattern of discipline in the home. A father who does not discipline his son is doing him a gross disfavor, a deep, serious deprivation.

Unfortunately, many fathers leave all or most of the discipline to the mothers, and this is wrong. A mother should only support and supplement the father's discipline. There is nothing that will wreck the endurance and peace of a home more than for a father and a mother to disagree on discipline. If father sets the standard for discipline in the home, (of course, we are not talking about abuse) and the mother tears it down by judging or neutralizing his discipline, this creates a wide open opportunity for Satan to invade that home.

"If you are not disciplined (and everyone undergoes discipline), then you are illegitimate children and not true sons" v.8. In other words, if a son is denied discipline; it is as though he is not a son at all; he is treated as one who is completely outside his family unit.

"Moreover, we have all had human fathers who disciplined us and we respected them for it" v.9. Discipline builds respect for the father. Mother teaches respect, primarily by example. She respects her husband, her children and her children's relationship with the father. Therefore, mother plays a very important role in fostering respect in the family. She either builds respect or tears it down.

"How much more should we submit to the Father of our spirits and live! Our fathers disciplined us for a little while..."v.9b,10a. The "little while" refers to the years we were growing up in the home. There eventually comes a time when a child outgrows and matures beyond family discipline, and he is by this time to have been trained to discipline himself.

It is tragic indeed if a child gets to that certain age when self-discipline should take over only to find that he has none. Parents, then, are unable to grant him commonplace freedoms, privileges and liberties lest he abuse them. If a child is not brought into self-discipline, then one might as well expect conflicts to arise and upheavals to invade the family.

"Our fathers disciplined us for a little while *as they thought best*" v.10, i.e., they did the best that they knew how, and made some mistakes, "but God disciplines us for our good, that we may share in his holiness" v.10b. Behold, it is not only the earthly father who disciplines us, for the Heavenly Father loves us, too, and He disciplines us.

God wants every son of His to mature in holiness of character and conduct. He is interested in the formation of a stable, wholesome personality. Yes, God disciplines us for our good. The earthly father desperately needs to submit to the Heavenly Father's discipline. In this way he becomes qualified to discipline his own children. What kind of example is he if he does not have discipline in his own life? How effectively can he discipline others if he has not submitted himself to the hand of God's discipline?

Young people and Children: If you refuse to let your parents discipline you, God will bring the discipline from somewhere else. If you drift out into the world, and have not yielded to those who are in authority over you to discipline you, then who is going to provide that discipline? Society will do it. How will they do it? Through mental hospitals, police, courts and penitentiaries.

If you protest, "You don't love me!", did you not accuse your parents of that? You will have become so unlovely that no one loves you. So, you will be treated in a different way.

Provide Love
There is something unique about God's Kingdom that makes it distinct and different from earthly rule. Every kingdom has government, sovereign rule, delegated authority and law, but God's Kingdom is a kingdom of love. Authority and discipline are administered in love.

Love is to family relationships what mortar is to a brick building; it is the ingredient that holds everything together in the face of every stormy trial that comes its way.

The world's concept of love is *eros* love: sensual, sexual and erotic. God, however, instructs men to display an entirely different kind of love: *agape* is the Greek word. This love is sacrificial, selfless love; its perfect expression is seen in Christ when He took the guilt of our sins and bore the penalty for them on the cross.

God commands: "Husbands, love your wives, just as Christ loved the church and gave himself up for her..." Eph. 5:25. *Agape* love may be accompanied by feelings, but it does not originate in the emotions. It is a love that seeks the welfare of others, and works no ill to any. Fathers show *agape* love for their children by obeying God's Word:

> Fathers, do not exasperate your children;
> instead, bring them up in the training and
> instruction of the Lord.   Eph. 6:4

136

Wives and mothers must also exhibit love in the home. In fact, the Word charges mature women in the church to "train the younger women to love their husbands and children" Titus 2:4. Interestingly, the love spoken of here is not *agape* but *phileo* which more accurately represents tender affection. It is an unselfish love which is ready to serve. *Phileo* love is characterized by faithfulness and devotedness. It cherishes its object with the greatest of priority. This is the pure love which women are challenged to have toward both husbands and children.

There is no substitute for love. Strong ties of family love are a bulwark against demon invasion; their absence is an open invitation to the devil to strike his most severe blow.

Finally, children are gifts from God, and they add greatly to the value of a family.

> Sons are a heritage from the Lord, children a
> reward from him. Like arrows in the hands
> of a warrior are sons born in one's youth.
> Blessed is the man whose quiver is full of
> them. They will not be put to shame when
> they contend with their enemies in the gate.
>
> Ps. 127:4-5

Children are God's gift and a sign of His favor. They are to be considered an inheritance, a reward; therefore, they are to be counted as blessings and not burdens: comforts and not crosses. Although a man says, "These are my children", in reality they are God's children, a stewardship trust from the Heavenly Father.

Parents are to have the same attitude toward their children as Christ had toward the twelve apostles. In His prayer to the Father, Jesus prayed: "They are yours; you gave them to me...I pray for them...those you have given me, for they are yours...While I was with them, I protected them and kept them safe" John 17:6, 9, 12.

The Psalmist compares children to "arrows". When in the making, arrows can be bent and straightened to make them serviceable, for they can be fashioned to fly straight and to hit the mark. God's glory is the mark we intend for our children. When children are once out of the hand, it is then too late to bend them. These "arrows" which were once "in the hand" can become arrows in the heart, a source of grief to godly parents.

Children brought up "in the training and instruction of the Lord" Eph. 6:4, will be an asset to the Kingdom of God and a threat to the kingdom of Satan. "They will not be put to shame when they contend with their enemies in the gate" Ps. 127:5b.

All your sons will be taught by the Lord, and great will be your children's peace.

Isa. 54:13

Jesus loves the little children;
All the children of the world.
Red and yellow, black and
white;
They are precious in His
sight.
Jesus loves the little children
of the world.

OTHER BOOKS
BY
FRANK & IDA MAE HAMMOND

CERDOS EN LA SALA

With more than 1 million copies in print, **Pigs In The Parlor** - the recognized handbook on Deliverance - is continuing to set people from around the world free from demonic bondage. This bestseller is also available in SPANISH!

Paperback **$7.95**

KINGDOM LIVING FOR THE FAMILY

A long awaited sequel to Pigs In The Parlor! Instead of offering unrealistic theories on raising families, Frank Hammond presents a practical plan for implementing divine order in the family, and helping prevent the need for deliverance.

Paperback **$7.95**

OVERCOMING REJECTION

Powerful help for confronting and dealing with rejection, a spirit that is so often the root cause for those seeking deliverance. This book will help you understand tools commonly employed by the enemy in his attacks on believers.

Paperback **$6.95**

Has shame maimed you?
Have you been crippled by embarrassment?
Or, have you merely had to battle being ashamed and
to fight the opinion of others?

The authors have found *shame* to not only be a root spirit that affects individuals from earliest childhood, but also to be bad fruit that may plague individuals throughout their lives.

Discover how you, or those you love, may live Shame Free!

$7.95+$3.95 Shipping
for 1st book, .40 each additional

Impact Christian Books
332 Leffingwell Ave., Suite 101, Kirkwood, MO 63122

A BLOOD COVENANT
IS THE MOST
SOLEMN, BINDING AGREEMENT POSSIBLE
BETWEEN TWO PARTIES.

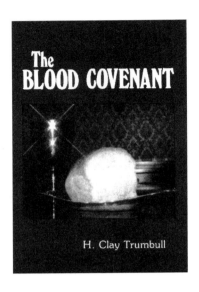

Perhaps one of the least understood, and yet most important and relevant factors necessary for an appreciation of the series of covenants and covenant relationships that our God has chosen to employ in His dealings with man, is the concept of the BLOOD COVENANT!

In this volume which has been "sold out," and "unavailable" for generations, lies truth which has blessed and will continue to bless every pastor, teacher, every serious Christian desiring to "go on with God."

Andrew Murray stated it beautifully years ago, when he said that if we were to but grasp the full knowledge of what God desires to do for us and understood the nature of His promises, it would "make the Covenant the very gate of heaven! May the Holy Spirit give us some vision of its glory."

$12.95 + 2.00 postage and handling

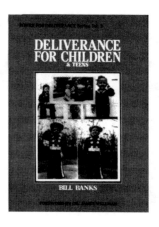

DELIVERANCE FOR CHILDREN & TEENS

The first practical handbook for ministering deliverance to children.

The material in this book is arranged to help parents in diagnosing their children's problems and in finding solutions for destructive behavior patterns.

The **Doorways** section of this book illustrates how demons enter, and how they take advantage of innocent, vulnerable children. More than a dozen categories of routes of entry are identified, and examples given!

The section on **Discipline** will be especially helpful to parents who wish to avoid problems, or remove them before they can become entrenched.

The **Mechanics of Ministry** section will help you, step by step, in ministering to a child needing help.

You will learn simple, surprising truths. For example...
* Easiest of all ministry is to small children! * Discipline is the most basic form of spiritual warfare and can bring deliverance!
* A child can acquire demonic problems through heredity or personal experience! * Deliverance need not be frightening if properly presented!

$6.95, Plus $1.50 Shipping

ABORTION'S AFTERMATH

Is There Hope of Healing?

What Are The True Effects of Abortion?

Read a dozen stories of women who suffered, and found freedom, from the various traumas associated with Abortion's aftermath...**Guilt**, **Shame**, **Torment**, **Miscarriage**, **Childlessness**, and even **Suicide**. Also discover the strategic steps and simple truths that have led these women, and hundreds more like them to be set free! *This book is full of hope, and this hope heals.*

> *"Millions of women have had an abortion: every one of them is a candidate for the ministry in this book."*

Ministering to Abortion's Aftermath   **$7.95**
by Bill & Sue Banks   Paperback   0-89228-057-3
        * *Plus $1.95 in shipping & handling*

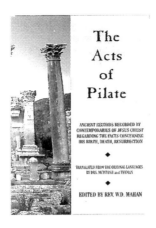

The
Acts
of
Pilate

ANCIENT RECORDS RECORDED BY
CONTEMPORARIES OF JESUS CHRIST
REGARDING THE FACTS CONCERNING
HIS BIRTH, DEATH, RESURRECTION

◆

TRANSLATED FROM THE ORIGINAL LANGUAGES
BY DRS. MCINTOSH and TWYMAN

◆

EDITED BY REV. W.D. MAHAN

This book was a favorite of the late Kathryn Kuhlman who often read from it on her radio show.

Early Church Writers such as Justin refer to the existence of these records, and Tertullian specifically mentions the report made by Pilate to the Emperor of Rome, Tiberius Caesar.

Chapters Include:
◆ *How These Records Were Discovered,*
◆ *A Short Sketch of the Talmuds,*
◆ *Constantine's Letter in Regard to Having Fifty Copies of the Scriptures Written and Bound,*
◆ *Jonathan's Interview with the Bethlehem Shepherds   Letter of Melker, Priest of the Synagogue at Bethlehem,*
◆ *Gamaliel's Interview with Joseph and Mary and Others Concerning Jesus,*
◆ *Report of Caiaphas to the Sanhedrim Concerning the Resurrection of Jesus,*
◆ *Valleus's Notes — "Acta Pilati," or Pilate's Report to Caesar of the Arrest, Trial, and Crucifixion of Jesus,*
◆ *Herod Antipater's Defense Before the Roman Senate in Regard to His Conduct At Bethlehem,*
◆ *Herod Antipas's Defense Before the Roman Senate in Regard to the Execution of John the Baptist,*
◆ *The Hillel Letters Regarding God's Providence to the Jews, by Hillel the Third*

THE ACTS OF PILATE $9.95, plus $2.00 Shipping

IMPACT CHRISTIAN BOOKS, INC.
332 Leffingwell Ave., Suite 101, Kirkwood, MO 63122

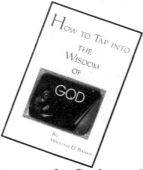

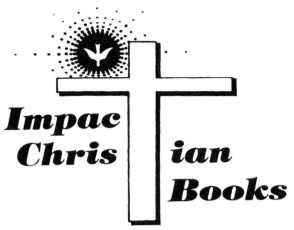

Impac Chris ian Books

332 Leffingwell Ave., Suite 101
Kirkwood, MO 63122

AVAILABLE AT YOUR LOCAL BOOKSTORE, OR YOU MAY
ORDER DIRECTLY. Toll-Free, order-line only M/C, DISC,
or VISA 1-800-451-2708.

Visit our Website at *www. impactchristianbooks.com*

Write for *FREE* Catalog.